1

THE SUNLIT PATH

The Sunlit Path

Passages from Conversations
and Writings of
THE MOTHER

Sri Aurobindo Ashram
Pondicherry, India

First Edition: 1984
Seventh Impression: 2001

ISBN 81-7058-025-0

© Sri Aurobindo Ashram Trust 1984
Published by Sri Aurobindo Ashram Publication Department
Printed at Sri Aurobindo Ashram Press, Pondicherry
PRINTED IN INDIA

PUBLISHER'S NOTE

The passages of this compilation have been selected from the Collected Works of the Mother. Almost all the passages have been taken from her conversations, a few from her writings. Details about the texts are given at the end of the book, as well as a glossary and a brief sketch of the Mother's life. The frontispiece is a photograph of the Mother on 5 July 1969, at the age of ninety-one.

A NOTE ABOUT PUNCTUATION

Closely spaced points (...) indicate a brief pause or hesitation in the Mother's speech. These suspension points – the equivalent of the French *points de suspension* – are used consistently in the Mother's Collected Works texts, from which the passages of this compilation have been taken.

Widely spaced points (. . .) indicate a deletion by the editor of some part of the text printed in the Collected Works. These ellipsis points have been used wherever there is any deletion of material from within an excerpted passage; for aesthetic reasons, these points have not been placed at the very beginning or end of passages in which they would otherwise occur.

CONTENTS

CONTENTS

Do not take my words for a teaching. Always they are a force in action, uttered with a definite purpose, and they lose their true power when separated from that purpose.

THE MOTHER

THE CALL

The Great Adventure

We are in a very special situation, extremely special, without precedent. We are now witnessing the birth of a new world; it is very young, very weak – not in its essence but in its outer manifestation – not yet recognised, not even felt, denied by the majority. But it is here. It is here, making an effort to grow, absolutely *sure* of the result. But the road to it is a completely new road which has never before been traced out – nobody has gone there, nobody has done that! It is a beginning, a *universal beginning*. So, it is an absolutely unexpected and unpredictable adventure.

There are people who love adventure. It is these I call, and I tell them this: "I invite you to the great adventure."

It is not a question of repeating spiritually what others have done before us, for our adventure begins beyond that. It is a question of a new creation, entirely new, with all the unforeseen events, the risks, the hazards it entails – a *real adventure*, whose goal is certain victory, but the road to which is unknown and must be traced out step by step in the unexplored. Something that has never been in this present universe and that will *never* be again in the same way. If that interests you... well, let us embark. What will happen to you tomorrow – I have no idea.

One must put aside all that has been foreseen, all that has been devised, all that has been constructed, and then... set off walking into the unknown. And – come what may! There.

The Sublimest of Adventures

There is a moment when life such as it is, the human consciousness such as it is, seems something absolutely impossible to bear, it creates a kind of disgust, repugnance; one says, "No, it is not that, it is not that; it can't be that, it can't continue." Well, when one comes to this, there is only to throw in one's *all* – all one's effort, all one's strength, all one's life, all one's being – into this chance, if you like, or this exceptional opportunity that is given to cross over to the other side. What a relief to set foot on the new path, that which will lead you elsewhere! This is worth the trouble of casting behind much luggage, of getting rid of many things in order to be able to take that leap. That's how I see the problem.

In fact it is the sublimest of adventures, and if one has in him in the slightest the true spirit of adventure, it is worth risking all for all.

A Decisive Turning-point

At the moment we are at a decisive turning-point in the history of the earth, once again. From every side I am asked, "What is going to happen?" Everywhere there is anguish, expectation, fear. "What is going to happen?..." There is only one reply: "If only man could consent to be spiritualised."

And perhaps it would be enough if some individuals became pure gold, for this would be enough to change the course of events.... We are faced with this necessity in a very urgent way.

This courage, this heroism which the Divine wants of us, why not use it to fight against one's own difficulties, one's own imperfections, one's own obscurities? Why not heroically face the furnace of inner purification so that it does not become necessary to pass once more through one of those terrible, gigantic destructions which plunge an entire civilisation into darkness?

This is the problem before us. It is for each one to solve it in his own way.

THE VALUE OF EDUCATION

One Dreams of Miracles

One dreams of miracles when one is young, one wants all wickedness to disappear, everything to be always luminous, beautiful, happy, one likes stories which end happily. This is what one should rely on. When the body feels its miseries, its limitations, one must establish this dream in it – of a strength which would have no limit, a beauty which would have no ugliness, and of marvellous capacities: one dreams of being able to rise into the air, of being wherever it is necessary to be, of setting things right when they go wrong, of healing the sick; indeed, one has all sorts of dreams when one is very young.... Usually parents or teachers pass their time throwing cold water on it, telling you, "Oh! it's a dream, it is not a reality." They should do the very opposite! Children should be taught, "Yes, this is what you must try to realise and not only is it possible but it is *certain* if you come in contact with the part in you which is capable of doing this thing. This is what should guide your life, organise it, make you develop in the direction of the *true reality* which the ordinary world calls illusion."

This is what it should be, instead of making children ordinary, with that dull, vulgar common sense which becomes an inveterate habit and, when something is going well, immediately brings up in the being the idea: "Oh, that won't last!", when somebody is kind, the impression, "Oh, he will change!", when one is capable of doing something, "Oh, tomorrow I won't be able to do it so well." This is like an acid, a destructive acid in the being, which takes away hope, certitude, confidence in future possibilities.

When a child is full of enthusiasm, never throw cold water on it, never tell him, "You know, life is not like that!" You should always encourage him, tell him, "Yes, at present things are not always like that, they *seem* ugly, but behind this there is a beauty that is trying to realise itself. This is what you should love and draw towards you, this is what you should make the object of your dreams, of your ambitions."

The Art of Living

Usually you are taught very few things – you are not taught even to sleep. People think that they have only to lie down in their bed and then they sleep. But this is not true! One must learn how to sleep as one must learn to eat, learn to do anything at all. And if one does not learn, well, one does it badly! Or one takes years and years to learn how to do it, and during all those years when it is badly done, all sorts of unpleasant things occur. And it is only after suffering much, making many mistakes, committing many stupidities, that, gradually, when one is old and has white hair, one begins to know how to do something. But if, when you were quite small, your parents or those who look after you, took the trouble to teach you how to do what you do, do it properly as it should be done, in the right way, then that would help you to avoid all – all these mistakes you make through the years. And not only do you make mistakes, but nobody tells you they are mistakes! And so you are surprised that you fall ill, are tired, don't know how to do what you want to, and that you have never been taught. Some children are not taught anything, and so they need years and years and years to learn the simplest things, even the most elementary thing: to be clean. . . .

   To live in the right way is a very difficult art, and unless one begins to learn it when quite young and to make an effort, one never knows it very well. Simply the art of keeping one's body in good health, one's mind quiet and goodwill in one's heart – things which are indispensable in order to live decently – I don't say in comfort, I don't say remarkably, I only say decently. Well, I don't think there are many who take care to teach this to their children.

One Needs Education

You think that you are sent to school, that you are made to do exercises, all this just for the pleasure of vexing you? Oh, no! It is because it's indispensable for you to have a frame in which you can learn how to form yourself. If you did your work of individualisation, of total formation, by yourself, all alone in a corner, nothing at all would be asked of you. But you don't do it, you wouldn't do it, there's not a single child who would do it, he wouldn't even know how to do it, where to begin. If a child were not taught how to live, he could not live, he wouldn't know how to do anything, anything. . . . If everyone had to go through the whole experience needed for the formation of an individuality, he would be long dead before having begun to live! This is the advantage of those – accumulated through centuries – who have had the experience and tell you, "Well, if you want to go quickly, to know in a few years what has been learnt through centuries, do this!" Read, learn, study and then, in the material field, you will be taught to do this in this way, that in that way, this again in this way (*gestures*). Once you know a little, you can find your own method, if you have the genius for it! But first one must stand on one's own feet and know how to walk. It is very difficult to learn it all alone. It's like that for everyone. One must form oneself. Therefore, one needs education.

Control Your Impulses

From the time you are quite young, the work of your educators is to teach you to control your impulses and obey only those which are in conformity with the laws under which you live or with the ideal you wish to follow or the customs of the environment in which you are. The value of this mental construction which will govern your impulses depends a great deal on the surroundings in which you live and the character of the parents or people who educate you. But whether it be good or bad, mediocre or excellent, it is always the result of a mental control over the impulses. When your parents tell you, "You should not do this", or when they say, "You have to do that", this is a beginning of education for the mind's control over the impulses.

Reason Must Be the Master

It is a good thing to begin to learn at an early age that to lead an efficient life and obtain from one's body the maximum it is able to give, reason must be the master of the house. And it is not a question of yoga or higher realisation, it is something which should be taught everywhere, in every school, every family, every home: man was made to be a mental being, and merely to be a man – we are not speaking of anything else, we are speaking only of being a man – life must be dominated by reason and not by vital impulses. This should be taught to all children from their infancy. . . . The first thing which should be taught to every human being as soon as he is able to think, is that he should obey reason which is a super-instinct of the species. Reason is the master of the nature of mankind. One must obey reason and absolutely refuse to be the slave of instincts. And here I am not talking to you about yoga, I am not talking about spiritual life, not at all; it has nothing to do with that. It is the basic wisdom of human life, purely human life: every human being who obeys anything other than reason is a kind of brute lower than the animal. That's all. And this should be taught everywhere; it is the basic education which should be given to children.

The reign of reason must come to an end only with the advent of the psychic law which manifests the divine Will.

Reason Is Developed by Using It

How can the reason be developed? . . .

Oh! by using it. Reason is developed like the muscles, like the will.

All these things are developed by a rational use. Reason! everyone possesses reason, only he doesn't make use of it. Some people are very much afraid of reason because it contradicts their impulses. So they prefer not to listen to it. Then, naturally, if one makes it a habit not to listen to reason, instead of developing, it loses its light more and more.

To develop reason you must want to do it sincerely; if on one side you tell yourself, "I want to develop my reason", and on the other you don't listen to what the reason tells you to do, then you never come to anything, because naturally, if each time it tells you, "Don't do this" or "Do this", you do the opposite, it will lose the habit of saying anything at all.

Education: Preparing the Consciousness

Usually all education, all culture, all refinement of the senses and the being is one of the best ways of curing instincts, desires, passions. To eliminate these things does not cure them; to cultivate, intellectualise, refine them, this is the surest means of curing. To give the greatest possible development for progress and growth, to acquire a certain sense of harmony and exactness of perception, this is a part of the culture of the being, of the education of the being. . . .

Education is certainly one of the best means of preparing the consciousness for a higher development. There are people with very crude and very simple natures, who can have great aspiration and attain a certain spiritual development, but the base will always be of an inferior quality, and as soon as they return to their ordinary consciousness they will find obstacles in it, because the stuff is too thin, there are not enough elements in their vital and material consciousness to enable them to bear the descent of a higher force.

A Child's Desires

Sweet Mother, how can we help a child to come out of this habit of always asking?

There are many ways. But first of all you must know whether you will not just stop him from freely expressing what he thinks and feels. Because this is what people usually do. They scold, even sometimes punish him; and so the child forms the habit of concealing his desires. But he is not cured of them. And you see, if he is always told, "No, you won't have that", then, simply, this state of mind gets settled in him: "Ah, when you are small, people don't give you anything! You must wait till you are big. When I am big I shall have all that I want." That's how it is. But this does not cure them. It is very difficult to bring up a child. There is a way which consists in giving him all he wants; and naturally, the next minute he will want something else, because that's the law, the law of desire: never to be satisfied. And so, if he is intelligent, one can tell him, "But you see, you insisted so much on having this and now you no longer care for it. You want something else." Yet if he was very clever he would answer, "Well, the best way of curing me is to give me what I ask for."

Some people cherish this idea all their life. When they are told that they should overcome their desires, they say, "The easiest way is to satisfy them." This kind of logic seems impeccable. But the fact is that it is not the object desired that has to be changed, it is the impulse of desire, the movement of desire. And for this a great deal of knowledge is needed, and this is difficult for a very young child. . . .

In fact, perhaps one should begin by shifting the movement to things which it is better to have from the true point of view, and which it is more difficult to obtain. If one could turn this impulse of desire towards a ... For example, when a child is full of desires, if one could give him a desire of a higher kind – instead of its being a desire for purely material objects, you understand, an altogether transitory satisfaction – if one could awaken in him the desire to know, the desire to learn, the desire to become a remarkable person... in this way, begin with that. As these things are difficult to do, so, gradually, he will develop his will for these things. Or even, from the material point of view, the desire to do something difficult, as for example, construct a toy which it is difficult to make – or give him a game of patience which requires a great deal of perseverance.

If one can orient them – it requires much discernment, much patience, but it can be done – and if one can orient them towards something like this, to succeed in very difficult games or to work out something which requires much care and attention, and can push them in some line like this so that it exercises a persevering will in them, then this can have results: turn their attention away from certain things and towards others. This needs constant care and it seems to be a way that's most – I can't say the easiest, for it is certainly not easy – but the most effective way.

True Need and Desire

It is very difficult to find the borderland between a true need and a desire. . . . And there we really face a problem which compels an extraordinary sincerity, for the very first way in which the vital meets life is through desire – and yet, there are necessities. But how to know if things are really necessary, not desired? . . . For that you must observe yourself very, very attentively, and if there is anything in you which produces something like a small intense vibration, then you may be sure that there lies a desire. For example, you say, "This food is necessary for me" – you believe, you imagine, you think that you need such and such a thing and you find the necessary means to obtain the thing. To know if it is a need or a desire, you must look at yourself very closely and ask yourself, "What will happen if I cannot get the thing?" Then if the immediate answer is, "Oh, it will be very bad", you may be sure that it is a matter of desire. It is the same for everything. For every problem you draw back, look at yourself and ask, "Let us see, am I

going to have the thing?" If at that moment something in you
jumps up with joy, you may be certain there is a desire. On the
other hand, if something tells you, "Oh, I am not going to get it",
and you feel very depressed, then again it is a desire.

Give up Desire

The Buddha has said that there is a greater joy in overcoming a
desire than in satisfying it. It is an experience everybody can have
and one that is truly very interesting, very interesting. . . .

There is a kind of inner communion with the psychic being
which takes place when one willingly gives up a desire, and
because of this one feels a much greater joy than if he had satisfied
his desire. Besides, most usually, almost without exception, when
one satisfies a desire it always leaves a kind of bitter taste
somewhere.

There is not one satisfied desire which does not give a kind of
bitterness; as when one has eaten too sugary a sweet it fills your
mouth with bitterness. It is like that. You must try sincerely.
Naturally you must not pretend to give up desire and keep it in a
corner, because then one becomes very unhappy. You must do it
sincerely.

Win Your Little Victories

If through an effort of inner consciousness and knowledge, you
can truly overcome in yourself a desire, that is to say, dissolve and
abolish it, and if through inner goodwill, through consciousness,
light, knowledge, you are able to dissolve the desire, you will be,
first of all in yourself personally, a hundred times happier than if
you had satisfied this desire, and then it will have a marvellous
effect. It will have a repercussion in the world of which you have
no idea. It will spread forth. For the vibrations you have created
will continue to spread. These things grow larger like the snow-

ball. The victory you win in your character, however small it be, is one which can be gained in the whole world. . . .

If you really want to do something good, the best thing you can do is to win your small victories in all sincerity, one after another, and thus you will do for the world the maximum you are able to.

Change Yourself First

You can do nothing with others unless you are able to do it with yourself. You can never give a good advice to anyone unless you are able to give it to yourself first, and to follow it. And if you see a difficulty somewhere, the best way of changing this difficulty is to change it in yourself first. If you see a defect in anyone, you may be sure it is in you, and you begin to change it in yourself. And when you will have changed it in yourself, you will be strong enough to change it in others. And this is a wonderful thing. People don't realise what an infinite grace it is that this universe is arranged in such a way that there is a collection of substance, from the most material to the highest spiritual, all that gathered together into what is called a small individual, but at the disposal of a central Will. And that is yours, your field of work, nobody can take it away from you, it is your own property. And to the extent you can work upon it, you will be able to have an action upon the world. But only to that extent. One must do more for oneself, besides, than one does for others.

MORALITY, RELIGION, YOGA

Spirituality and Morality

[There is a] great difference between spirituality and morality, two things that are constantly confused with each other. The spiritual life, the life of Yoga, has for its object to grow into the divine consciousness and for its result to purify, intensify, glorify and perfect what is in you. It makes you a power for manifesting the Divine; it raises the character of each personality to its full value and brings it to its maximum expression; for this is part of the Divine plan. Morality proceeds by a mental construction and, with a few ideas of what is good and what is not, sets up an ideal type into which all must force themselves. This moral ideal differs in its constituents and its ensemble at different times and different places. And yet it proclaims itself as a unique type, a categoric absolute; it admits of none other outside itself; it does not even admit a variation within itself. All are to be moulded according to its single ideal pattern, everybody is to be made uniformly and faultlessly the same. It is because morality is of this rigid unreal nature that it is in its principle and its working the contrary of the spiritual life. The spiritual life reveals the one essence in all, but reveals too its infinite diversity; it works for diversity in oneness and for perfection in that diversity. Morality lifts up one artificial standard contrary to the variety of life and the freedom of the spirit. Creating something mental, fixed and limited, it asks all to conform to it. All must labour to acquire the same qualities and the same ideal nature. Morality is not divine or of the Divine; it is of man and human. Morality takes for its basic element a fixed division into the good and the bad; but this is an arbitrary notion. It takes things that are relative and tries to impose them as absolutes; for this good and this bad differ in differing climates and times, epochs and countries. The moral notion goes so far as to say that there are good desires and bad desires and calls on you to accept the one and reject the other. But the spiritual life demands that you should reject desire altogether. Its law is that you must cast aside all movements that draw you away from the Divine. You must reject them, not because they are bad in themselves, – for they may be good for another man or in another sphere, – but because they belong to the impulses or forces that, being unillumined and ignorant, stand in the way of your approach to the Divine. All desires, whether good or bad, come within this description; for desire itself arises from an unillumined vital being and its ignorance. On the other hand you must accept all movements that bring you into contact with the Divine. But you accept them, not because they are good in themselves, but because they bring you to the Divine. Accept then all that takes you to the Divine. Reject all that takes you away from it, but do not say that this is good and that is bad or try to impose your outlook on others; for, what you term bad may be the very thing that is good for your neighbour who is not trying to realise the Divine Life.

Hasn't Morality Helped?

Sweet Mother, hasn't morality helped us to increase our consciousness?

That depends on people. There are people who are helped by it, there are people who are not helped *at all*.

Morality is something altogether artificial and arbitrary, and in most cases, among the best, it checks the true spiritual effort by a sort of moral satisfaction that one is on the right path and a true gentleman, that one does one's duty, fulfils all the moral requirements of life. Then one is so self-satisfied that one no longer moves or makes any progress.

It is very difficult for a virtuous man to enter the path of God; this has been said very often, but it is altogether true, for he is *most* self-satisfied, he thinks he has realised what he ought to have realised, he no longer has either the aspiration or even that elementary humility which makes one want to progress. You see, one who is known here as a sattwic man is usually very comfortably settled in his own virtue and never thinks of coming out of it. So, that puts you a million leagues away from the divine realisation.

What really helps, until one has found the inner light, is to make for oneself a certain number of rules which naturally should not be too rigid and fixed, but yet should be precise enough to prevent one from going completely out of the right path or making irreparable mistakes – mistakes the consequences of which one suffers all one's life.

To do that, it,is good to set up a certain number of principles in oneself, which, however, should be for each one, in conformity with his own nature. If you adopt a social, collective rule, you immediately make yourself a slave to this social rule, and that prevents you almost radically from making any effort for transformation.

Serving Humanity

Why do you want to serve humanity, what is your idea? It is ambition, it is in order to become a great man among men. It is difficult to understand?... I can see that!

The Divine is everywhere. So if one serves humanity, one serves the Divine, isn't that so?

That's marvellous! The clearest thing in this business is to say: "The Divine is in me. If I serve myself, I am also serving the Divine!" (*Laughter*) In fact, the Divine is everywhere. The Divine will do His own work very well without you.

I see quite well that you do not understand. But truly, if you do understand that the Divine is there, in all things, with what are you meddling in serving humanity? To serve humanity you must know better than the Divine what must be done for it. Do you know better than the Divine how to serve it?

The Divine is everywhere. Yes. Things don't seem to be Divine.... As for me, I see only one solution: if you want to help humanity, there is only one thing to do, it is to take yourself as completely as possible and offer yourself to the Divine. That is the solution. Because in this way, at least the material reality which you represent will be able to grow a little more like the Divine.

We are told that the Divine is in all things. Why don't things change? Because the Divine does not get a response, everything does not respond to the Divine. One must search the depths of the consciousness to see this. What do you want to do to serve humanity? Give food to the poor? – You can feed millions of them. That will not be a solution, this problem will remain the same. Give new and better living conditions to men? – The Divine is in them, how is it that things don't change? The Divine must know better than you the condition of humanity. What are you? You represent only a little bit of consciousness and a little bit of matter, it is that you call "myself". If you want to help humanity, the world or the universe, the only thing to do is to give that little bit entirely to the Divine. Why is the world not divine?... It is evident that the world is not in order. So the only solution to the problem is to give what belongs to you. Give it totally, entirely to the Divine; not only for yourself but for humanity, for the universe. There is no better solution. How do you want to help humanity? You don't even know what it needs. Perhaps you know still less what power you are serving. How can you change anything without indeed having changed yourself?

In any case, you are not powerful enough to do it. How do you expect to help another if you do not have a higher consciousness than he? It is such a childish idea! It is children who say: "I am opening a boarding-house, I am going to build a crèche, give soup to the poor, preach this knowledge, spread this religion. . . ." It is only because you consider yourself better than others, think you know better than they what they should be or do. That's what it is, serving humanity. You want to continue all that? It has not changed things much. It is not to help humanity that one opens a hospital or a school. . . .

You may open millions of hospitals, that will not prevent people getting ill. On the contrary, they will have every facility and encouragement to fall ill. We are steeped in ideas of this kind. This puts your conscience at rest: "I have come to the world, I must help others." One tells oneself: "How disinterested I am! I am going to help humanity." All this is nothing but egoism.

In fact, the first human being that concerns you is yourself. You want to diminish suffering, but unless you can change the capacity of suffering into a certitude of being happy, the world will not change. It will always be the same, we turn in a circle – one civilisation follows another, one catastrophe another; but the thing does not change, for there is something missing, something not there, that is the consciousness. That's all.

Religion

Religion belongs to the higher mind of humanity. It is the effort of man's higher mind to approach, as far as lies in its power, something beyond it, something to which humanity gives the name God or Spirit or Truth or Faith or Knowledge or the Infinite, some kind of Absolute, which the human mind cannot reach and yet tries to reach. Religion may be divine in its ultimate origin; in its actual nature it is not divine but human. In truth we should speak rather of religions than of religion; for the religions made by man are many. . . .

The first and principal article of these established and formal religions runs always, "Mine is the supreme, the only truth, all others are in falsehood or inferior." For without this fundamental dogma, established credal religions could not have existed. If you do not believe and proclaim that you alone possess the one or the highest truth, you will not be able to impress people and make them flock to you.

This attitude is natural to the religious mind; but it is just that which makes religion stand in the way of the spiritual life. The articles and dogmas of a religion are mind-made things and, if you cling to them and shut yourself up in a code of life made out for you, you do not know and cannot know the truth of the Spirit that lies beyond all codes and dogmas, wide and large and free. When you stop at a religious creed and tie yourself in it, taking it for the only truth in the world, you stop the advance and widening of your inner soul. But if you look at religion from another angle, it need not always be an obstacle to all men. If you regard it as one of the higher activities of humanity and if you can see in it the aspirations of man without ignoring the imperfection of all man-made things, it may well be a kind of help for you to approach the spiritual life. Taking it up in a serious and earnest spirit, you can try to find out what truth is there, what aspiration lies hidden in it, what divine inspiration has undergone transformation and deformation here by the human mind and a human organisation, and with an appropriate mental stand you can get religion even as it is to throw some light on your way and to lend some support to your spiritual endeavour.

Yoga and Religion

Sweet Mother, what is the difference between yoga and religion?

Ah! my child... it is as though you were asking me the difference between a dog and a cat!

(Long silence)

Imagine someone who, in some way or other, has heard of something like the Divine or has a personal feeling that something of the kind exists, and begins to make all sorts of efforts: efforts of will, of discipline, efforts of concentration, all sorts of efforts to find this Divine, to discover what He is, to become acquainted with Him and unite with Him. Then this person is doing yoga.

Now, if this person has noted down all the processes he has used and constructs a fixed system, and sets up all that he has discovered as absolute laws – for example, he says: the Divine is like this, to find the Divine you must do this, make this particular

gesture, take this attitude, perform this ceremony, and you must
admit that *this* is the truth, you must say, "I accept that this is the
Truth and I fully adhere to it; and your method is the only right
one, the only one which exists" – if all that is written down,
organised, arranged into fixed laws and ceremonies, it becomes a
religion.

Sri Aurobindo's Teaching and Religion

*Many people say that the teaching of Sri Aurobindo is a new
religion. Would you say that it is a religion?*

People who say that are fools who don't even know what they are
talking about. You only have to read all that Sri Aurobindo has
written to know that it is impossible to base a religion on his works,
because he presents each problem, each question in all its aspects,
showing the truth contained in each way of seeing things, and he
explains that in order to attain the Truth you must realise a
synthesis which goes beyond all mental notions and emerge into a
transcendence beyond thought. . . .

I repeat that when we speak of Sri Aurobindo there can be no
question of a teaching nor even of a revelation, but of an action
from the Supreme; no religion can be founded on that.

But men are so foolish that they can change anything into a
religion, so great is their need of a fixed framework for their
narrow thought and limited action. They do not feel secure unless
they can assert this is true and that is not; but such an assertion
becomes impossible for anyone who has read and understood
what Sri Aurobindo has written. Religion and Yoga do not belong
to the same plane of being and spiritual life can exist in all its purity
only when it is free from all mental dogma.

The Resolution to Do Yoga

You see, one may have a very good will, a life oriented towards a divine realisation, in any case a more or less superficial consecration to a divine work, *and not do yoga.*

To do Sri Aurobindo's yoga is to want to transform oneself integrally, it is to have a single aim in life, such that nothing else exists any longer, that alone exists. And so one feels it clearly in oneself whether one wants it or not; but if one doesn't, one can still have a life of goodwill, a life of service, of understanding; one can labour for the Work to be accomplished more easily – all that – one can do many things. But between this and doing yoga there is a great difference.

And to do yoga you must want it consciously, you must know what it is, to begin with. You must know what it is, you must take a resolution about it; but once you have taken the resolution, you must no longer flinch. That is why you must take it in full knowledge of the thing. You must know what you are deciding upon when you say, "I want to do yoga"; and that is why I don't think I have ever pressed you from this point of view. . . .

But the day you make a choice – when you have done it in all sincerity and have felt within yourself a radical decision – the thing is different. There is the light and the path to be followed, quite straight, and you must not deviate from it. It fools no one, you know; yoga is not a joke. You must know what you are doing when you choose it. But when you choose it, you must hold on to it. You have no longer the right to vacillate. You must go straight ahead. There! . . .

To do the yoga, this yoga of transformation which, of all things, is the most arduous – it is only if one feels that one has come here for that (I mean here upon earth) and that one has to do nothing else but that, and that it is the only reason of one's existence – even if one has to toil hard, suffer, struggle, it is of no importance – "This is what I want, and nothing else" – then it is different. Otherwise I shall say, "Be happy and be good, and that's all that is asked of you. Be good, in the sense of being understanding, knowing that the conditions in which you have lived arc exceptional, and try to live a higher, more noble, more true life than the ordinary one, so as to allow a little of this consciousness, this light and its goodness to express itself in the world. It would be very good." There we are.

But once you have set foot on the path of yoga, you must have a resolution of steel and walk straight on to the goal, whatever the cost.

A Call for the Path

What do you want the Yoga for? To get power? To attain to peace and calm? To serve humanity?

None of these motives is sufficient to show that you are meant for the Path.

The question you are to answer is this: Do you want the Yoga for the sake of the Divine? Is the Divine the supreme fact of your life, so much so that it is simply impossible for you to do without it? Do you feel that your very *raison d'être* is the Divine and without it there is no meaning in your existence? If so, then only can it be said that you have a call for the Path.

This is the first thing necessary – aspiration for the Divine.

The next thing you have to do is to tend it, to keep it always alert and awake and living. And for that what is required is concentration – concentration upon the Divine with a view to an integral and absolute consecration to its Will and Purpose.

Concentrate in the heart. Enter into it; go within and deep and far, as far as you can. Gather all the strings of your consciousness that are spread abroad, roll them up and take a plunge and sink down.

A fire is burning there, in the deep quietude of the heart. It is the divinity in you – your true being. Hear its voice, follow its dictates.

SURRENDER, SELF-OFFERING, HUMILITY

Two Paths of Yoga

There are two paths of Yoga, one of *tapasyā* (discipline), and the other of surrender. The path of *tapasyā* is arduous. Here you rely solely upon yourself, you proceed by your own strength. You ascend and achieve according to the measure of your force. There is always the danger of falling down. And once you fall, you lie broken in the abyss and there is hardly a remedy. The other path, the path of surrender, is safe and sure. It is here, however, that the Western people find their difficulty. They have been taught to fear and avoid all that threatens their personal independence. They have imbibed with their mothers' milk the sense of individuality. And surrender means giving up all that. In other words, you may follow, as Ramakrishna says, either the path of the baby monkey or that of the baby cat. The baby monkey holds to its mother in order to be carried about and it must hold firm, otherwise if it loses its grip, it falls. On the other hand, the baby cat does not hold to its mother, but is held by the mother and has no fear nor responsibility; it has nothing to do but to let the mother hold it and cry *ma ma*.

Surrender and the Yoga

Surrender is the decision taken to hand over the responsibility of your life to the Divine. Without this decision nothing is at all possible; if you do not surrender, the Yoga is entirely out of the question. Everything else comes naturally after it, for the whole process starts with surrender. You can surrender either through knowledge or through devotion. You may have a strong intuition that the Divine alone is the truth and a luminous conviction that without the Divine you cannot manage. Or you may have a spontaneous feeling that this line is the only way of being happy, a strong psychic desire to belong exclusively to the Divine: "I do not belong to myself," you say, and give up the responsibility of your being to the Truth. Then comes self-offering: "Here I am, a creature of various qualities, good and bad, dark and enlightened. I offer myself as I am to you, take me up with all my ups and downs, conflicting impulses and tendencies – do whatever you like with me."

True Surrender Enlarges You

By surrender we mean. . . a spontaneous self-giving, a giving of all your self to the Divine, to a greater Consciousness of which you are a part. Surrender will not diminish, but increase; it will not lessen or weaken or destroy your personality, it will fortify and aggrandise it. Surrender means a free total giving with all the delight of the giving; there is no sense of sacrifice in it. If you have the slightest feeling that you are making a sacrifice, then it is no longer surrender. For it means that you reserve yourself or that you are trying to give, with grudging or with pain and effort, and have not the joy of the gift, perhaps not even the feeling that you are giving. When you do anything with the sense of a compression of your being, be sure that you are doing it in the wrong way. True surrender enlarges you; it increases your capacity; it gives you a greater measure in quality and in quantity which you could not have had by yourself. This new greater measure of quality and quantity is different from anything you could attain before: you enter into another world, into a wideness which you could not have entered if you did not surrender. It is as when a drop of water falls into the sea; if it still kept there its separate identity, it would remain a little drop of water and nothing more, a little drop crushed by all the immensity around, because it has not surrendered. But, surrendering, it unites with the sea and participates in the nature and power and vastness of the whole sea.

The Most Important Surrender

The most important surrender is the surrender of your character, your way of being, so that it may change. If you do not surrender your very own nature, never will this nature change. It is this that is most important. You have certain ways of understanding, certain ways of reacting, certain ways of feeling, almost certain ways of progressing, and above all, a special way of looking at life and expecting from it certain things – well, it is this you must surrender. That is, if you truly want to receive the divine Light and transform yourself, it is your whole way of being you must offer – offer by opening it, making it as receptive as possible so that the divine Consciousness which sees how you ought to be, may act directly and change all these movements into movements more true, more in keeping with your real truth. This is infinitely more important than surrendering what one does.

It is not what one does (what one does is very important, that's evident) that is the most important thing but what one *is*. Whatever the activity, it is not quite the way of doing it but the state of consciousness in which it is done that is important. You may work, do disinterested work without any idea of personal profit, work for the joy of working, but if you are not at the same time ready to leave this work, to change the work or change the way of working, if you cling to your own way of working, your surrender is not complete. You must come to a point when everything is done because you feel within, very clearly, in a more and more imperious way, that it is this which must be done and in this particular way, and that you do it only because of that. You do not do it because of any habit, attachment or preference, nor even any conception, even a preference for the idea that it is the best thing to do – else your surrender is not total.

Yoga Is Effected through Offering

Yoga means union with the Divine, and the union is effected through offering – it is founded on the offering of yourself to the Divine. In the beginning you start by making this offering in a general way, as though once for all; you say, "I am the servant of the Divine; my life is given absolutely to the Divine; all my efforts are for the realisation of the Divine Life." But that is only the first step; for this is not sufficient. When the resolution has been taken, when you have decided that the whole of your life shall be given to the Divine, you have still at every moment to remember it and carry it out in all the details of your existence. You must feel at every step that you belong to the Divine; you must have the constant experience that, in whatever you think or do, it is always the Divine Consciousness that is acting through you. You have no longer anything that you can call your own; you feel everything as coming from the Divine, and you have to offer it back to its source. When you can realise that, then even the smallest thing to which you do not usually pay much attention or care, ceases to be trivial and insignificant; it becomes full of meaning and it opens up a vast horizon beyond.

This is what you have to do to carry out your general offering in detailed offerings. Live constantly in the presence of the Divine; live in the feeling that it is this presence which moves you and is doing everything you do. Offer all your movements to it, not only every mental action, every thought and feeling but even the most ordinary and external actions such as eating; when you eat, you must feel that it is the Divine who is eating through you. When you can thus gather all your movements into the One Life, then you have in you unity instead of division. No longer is one part of your nature given to the Divine, while the rest remains in its ordinary ways, engrossed in ordinary things; your entire life is taken up, an integral transformation is gradually realised in you.

In the integral Yoga, the integral life down even to the smallest detail has to be transformed, to be divinised. There is nothing here that is insignificant, nothing that is indifferent. You cannot say,

"When I am meditating, reading philosophy or listening to these conversations I will be in this condition of an opening towards the Light and call for it, but when I go out to walk or see friends I can allow myself to forget all about it." To persist in this attitude means that you will remain untransformed and never have the true union; always you will be divided; you will have at best only glimpses of this greater life. For although certain experiences and realisations may come to you in meditation or in your inner consciousness, your body and your outer life will remain un-changed. An inner illumination that does not take any note of the body and the outer life, is of no great use, for it leaves the world as it is.

Empty Contemplation

I have never seen people who have left everything in order to go and sit down in a more or less empty contemplation (for it is more or less empty), I have never seen such people making any progress, or in any case their progress is very trifling. I have seen persons who had no pretensions of doing yoga, who were simply filled with enthusiasm by the idea of terrestrial transformation and of the descent of the Divine into the world and who did their little bit of work with that enthusiasm in the heart, giving themselves wholly, without reserve, without any selfish idea of a personal salvation; these I have seen making magnificent progress, truly magnificent. And sometimes they are wonderful. I have seen sannyasis, I have seen people who live in monasteries, I have seen people who professed to be yogis, well, I would not exchange one of the others for a dozen such people. . . . It is not by running away from the world that you will change it. It is by working there, modestly, humbly but with a fire in the heart, something that burns like an offering.

Ascetic Methods

Mother, for self-mastery are not the ascetic methods useful sometimes?

No! You cure nothing. You only give yourself the illusion that you have progressed, but you cure nothing. The proof is that if you stop your ascetic methods, the thing is even stronger than before; it comes back with a vengeance. It depends upon what you call ascetic methods. If it is not to indulge in satisfying all your desires, this indeed is not asceticism, it is common sense. It is something else. Ascetic methods are things like repeated fasting, compelling yourself to endure the cold... in fact, to torture your body a little. This indeed gives you only a spiritual pride, nothing more. It masters nothing at all. It is infinitely easier. People do it because it is very easy, it is simple. Just because the pride is quite satisfied and the vanity can get puffed up, it becomes very easy. One makes a great demonstration of his ascetic virtues, and so considers himself an extremely important personage, and that helps him to endure many things.

It is much more difficult to master one's impulses quietly, composedly, and to prevent them from showing themselves – much more! – without taking ascetic measures. It is much more difficult not to be attached to the things you possess than to possess nothing. This is something that has been known for centuries. It requires a much greater quality not to be attached to the things one possesses than to be without any possessions or to reduce one's possessions to a strict minimum. It is much more difficult. It is a much higher degree of moral worth. Simply this attitude: when a thing comes to you, to take it, use it; when for one reason or another it goes away, to let it go and not regret it. Not to refuse it when it comes, to know how to adapt yourself and not to regret it when it goes.

Outer Discipline

But doesn't some outer discipline help?

If you impose a discipline upon yourself and if it isn't too stupid, it may help you. A discipline, I tell you – disciplines, tapasyas, all ascetic disciplines are, as ordinarily practised, the best means of making you proud, of building up in you such a terrific pride that never, never will you be converted. It will have to be broken down with hammer-strokes.

The first condition is a healthy humility which makes you realise that unless you are sustained, nourished, helped, enlightened, guided by the Divine, you are *nothing at all*. There now. When you have felt that, not only understood it with your mind, but felt it down to your very body, then you will begin to be wise, but not before.

True Humility

What is the right and the wrong way of being humble?

It is very simple, when people are told "be humble", they think immediately of "being humble before other men" and that humility is wrong. True humility is humility before the Divine, that is, a precise, exact, *living* sense that one is nothing, one can do nothing, understand nothing without the Divine, that even if one is exceptionally intelligent and capable, this is nothing in comparison with the divine Consciousness, and this sense one must always keep, because then one always has the true attitude of receptivity – a humble receptivity that does not put personal pretensions in opposition to the Divine.

Someone Who Knows Very Little

It is not necessarily someone with experience who is most advanced. He lacks an element of simplicity, modesty, and the plasticity that comes from the fact that one is not yet totally developed. As one grows, something crystallises in the head; it gets more and more fixed and unless you try very hard you finish by becoming fossilised. This is what usually happens to people, particularly those who have tried for some realisation and succeeded in it or those who have come to believe they have reached the goal. In any case, it was their personal goal. They have reached it, they have attained. It is done, they remain there; they settle there, they say "that's it." And they do no more any more. So, after that they may live ten years more, or twenty or thirty, they will not budge. They are there, they will stay there. Such people lack all the suppleness of stuff that's necessary for going further and progressing. They are stuck. They are very good objects to be put in a museum, but not for doing work. They are like samples to show what can be done but they are not the stuff to do more. For me personally, I admit I prefer for my work someone who knows very little, has not laboured too much, but who has a great deal of aspiration, a great goodwill and who feels in himself this flame, this need for progressing. He may know very little, may have realised still less, but if he has that within him, it is good stuff with which one can go very far, much further.

Open Yourself, Be Modest

What you should do is to throw the doors of your being wide open to the Divine. The moment you conceal something, you step straight into Falsehood. The least suppression on your part pulls you immediately down into unconsciousness. If you want to be fully conscious, be always in front of the Truth – completely open yourself and try your utmost to let it see deep inside you, into every corner of your being. That alone will bring into you light and consciousness and all that is most true. Be absolutely modest – that is to say, know the distance between what you are and what is to be, not allowing the crude physical mentality to think that it knows when it does not, that it can judge when it cannot. Modesty implies the giving up of yourself to the Divine whole-heartedly, asking for help and, by submission, winning the freedom and absence of responsibility which imparts to the mind utter quietness. Not otherwise can you hope to attain the union with the Divine Consciousness and the Divine Will.

SINCERITY, WEAKNESS, WILL-POWER

Sincerity

What is the fundamental virtue to be cultivated in order to prepare for the spiritual life?

I have said this many times, but this is an opportunity to repeat it: it is *sincerity*.

A sincerity which must become total and absolute, for sincerity *alone* is your protection on the spiritual path. If you are not sincere, at the very next step you are sure to fall and break your head. All kinds of forces, wills, influences, entities are there, on the look-out for the least little rift in this sincerity and they immediately rush in through that rift and begin to throw you into confusion.

Therefore, before doing anything, beginning anything, trying anything, be sure *first of all* that you are not only as sincere as you can be, but have the intention of becoming still more so.

For that is your only protection.

Perfect Sincerity

Fundamentally, whatever be the path one follows – whether the path of surrender, consecration, knowledge – if one wants it to be perfect, it is always equally difficult, and there is but one way, one only, I know of only one: that is perfect sincerity, but *perfect* sincerity!

Do you know what perfect sincerity is?...

Never to try to deceive oneself, never let any part of the being try to find out a way of convincing the others, never to explain favourably what one does in order to have an excuse for what one wants to do, never to close one's eyes when something is unpleasant, never to let anything pass, telling oneself, "That is not important, next time it will be better."

Oh! it is very difficult. Just try for one hour and you will see how very difficult it is. Only one hour, to be *totally, absolutely* sincere. To let nothing pass. That is, all one does, all one feels, all one thinks, all one wants, is *exclusively* the Divine.

"I want nothing but the Divine, I think of nothing but the Divine, I do nothing but what will lead me to the Divine, I love nothing but the Divine."

Try – try, just to see, try for half an hour, you will see how difficult it is!

Unhappiness and Insincerity

You feel uneasy, very miserable, dejected, a bit unhappy: "Things are not quite pleasant today. They are the same as they were yesterday; yesterday they were marvellous, today they are not pleasing!" – Why? Because yesterday you were in a perfect state of surrender, more or less perfect – and today you aren't any more. So, what was so beautiful yesterday is no longer beautiful today. That joy you had within you, that confidence, the assurance that all will be well and the great Work will be accomplished, that certitude – all this, you see, has become veiled, has been replaced by a kind of doubt and, yes, by a discontent: "Things are not beautiful, the world is nasty, people are not pleasant." It goes sometimes to this length: "The food is not good, yesterday it was excellent." It is the same but today it is not good! This is the barometer! You may immediately tell yourself that an insincerity has crept in somewhere. It is very easy to know, you don't need to be very learned, for, as Sri Aurobindo has said in *Elements of Yoga*: One knows whether one is happy or unhappy, one knows whether one is content or discontented, one doesn't need to ask oneself, put complicated questions for this, one knows it! – Well, it is very simple.

The moment you feel unhappy, you may write beneath it: "I am not sincere!" These two sentences go together:

"I FEEL UNHAPPY."
"I AM NOT SINCERE."

Now, what is it that is wrong? Then one begins to take a look, it is easy to find out...

The Psychic Mirror

This is life. One stumbles and falls on the first occasion. One tells oneself: "Oh! one can't always be so serious", and when the other part returns, once again, one repents bitterly: "I was a fool, I have wasted my time, now I must begin again...." At times there is one part that's ill-humoured, in revolt, full of worries, and another which is progressive, full of surrender. All that, one after the other.

There is but one remedy: the signpost must always be there, a mirror well placed in one's feelings, impulses, all one's sensations. One sees them in this mirror. There are some which are not very beautiful or pleasant to look at; there are others which are beautiful, pleasant, and must be kept. This one does a hundred times a day if necessary. And it is very interesting. One draws a kind of big circle around the psychic mirror and arranges all the elements around it. If there is something that is not all right, it casts a sort of grey shadow upon the mirror: this element must be shifted, organised. It must be spoken to, made to understand, one must come out of that darkness. If you do that, you never get bored.

Bad Impulses and Thoughts

Mother, when we come to you, we try to be at our best possible, that is, to have very good thoughts; but often, on the contrary, all the bad impulses, bad thoughts we had during the day come forward.

That is perhaps so that you can get rid of them.

If they come, one can offer them and ask to be rid of them.

That perhaps is the reason, it is because the Consciousness acts for purification. It is no use at all hiding things and pushing them behind, like this, and imagining they are not there because one has put a veil in front. It is much better to see oneself as one is – provided one is ready to give up this way of being. If you come allowing all the bad movements to rise to the surface, to show themselves; if you offer them, if you say, "Well, this is how I am", and if at the same time you have the aspiration to be different, then this second of presence is extremely useful; you can, yes, in a few seconds receive the help you need to get rid of them; while if you come like a little saint and go away content, without having received anything, it is not very useful.

Automatically the Consciousness acts like that, it is like the ray that brings light where there wasn't any. Only, what is needed is to be in a state where one *wants* to give up the thing, to get rid of it – not to cling to it and keep it. If one sincerely wants to pull it out of oneself, make it disappear, then it is very useful.

Offer the Wrong Movements

Instead of driving [a wrong movement] underground, it is to be offered. It is to place the thing, the movement itself, to *project* it into the light.... Generally it wriggles and refuses! But (*Mother laughs*) that is the only way. That is why this Consciousness is so precious.... Well, what brings about the suppression is the idea of good and bad, a kind of contempt or shame for what is considered bad, and you do like this (*gesture of repulsion*), you do not want to see it, you do not want it to be there. It must... The first thing – the very first thing to realise is that it is the weakness of our consciousness that makes this division and that there is a Consciousness (now I am sure of it) in which that does not exist, in which what we call "evil" is as much necessary as what we call "good", and that if we can project our sensation – or our activity or our perception – into that Light, that will bring the cure. Instead of suppressing or rejecting it as something to be destroyed (it cannot be destroyed!), it has to be projected into the Light. And because of this I have had for several days a very interesting experience: instead of seeking to throw away far from oneself certain things (which one does not accept, and which produce an imbalance in the being), instead of doing that, to accept them, take them as part of oneself and... (*Mother opens her hands*) offer them up. They do not want to be offered, but there is a way of compelling them: the resistance is diminished in the proportion as we can diminish in us our sense of disapprobation; if we can replace this sense of disapprobation by a higher understanding, then we succeed. It is much more easy.

I believe it is that. All, all the movements that drag you down must be put in contact with the higher understanding.

The Positive and Negative Sides

There is a positive and a negative side to this work.

The positive side is to increase one's aspiration, develop one's consciousness, unify one's being, to go within in order to enter more and more into contact with one's psychic being; to take up all the parts, all the movements, all the activities of one's being and put them before this psychic consciousness so that they fall into their true place in relation to this centre; finally, to organise all one's aspiration towards the Divine and one's progress towards the Divine. That is the positive side.

At the same time the negative side consists in refusing methodically and with discernment all the influences which come from outside or from the subconscient or inconscient or from the environment, and stand in the way of spiritual progress. One must discern these influences, suggestions, impulses, and systematically refuse them without ever getting discouraged by their persistence and ever yielding to their will. One must, at the same time, observe clearly in one's being all its different elements, obscure, egoistic, unconscious, or even ill-willed, which consciously or otherwise, answer these bad influences, and allow them not only to penetrate into the consciousness, but sometimes to get settled there. That is the negative side.

Both must be practised at the same time. According to the moment, the occasion, the inner readiness, you must insist now on one, now on the other, but never forget either of them.

Vigilance

Vigilance means to be awake, to be on one's guard, to be sincere – never to be taken by surprise. When you want to do sadhana, at each moment of your life, there is a choice between taking a step that leads to the goal and falling asleep or sometimes even going backwards, telling yourself, "Oh, later on, not immediately" – sitting down on the way.

To be vigilant is not merely to resist what pulls you downward, but above all to be alert in order not to lose any opportunity to progress, any opportunity to overcome a weakness, to resist a temptation, any opportunity to learn something, to correct something, to master something. If you are vigilant, you can do in a few days what would otherwise take years. If you are vigilant, you change each circumstance of your life, each action, each movement into an occasion for coming nearer the goal.

Refuse the Lower Movements

Sweet Mother, how can we empty the consciousness of its mixed contents?

By aspiration, the rejection of the lower movements, a call to a higher force. If you do not accept certain movements, then naturally, when they find that they can't manifest, gradually they diminish in force and stop occurring. If you refuse to express everything that is of a lower kind, little by little the very thing disappears, and the consciousness is emptied of lower things. It is by refusing to give expression – I mean not only in action but also in thought, in feeling. When impulses, thoughts, emotions come, if you refuse to express them, if you push them aside and remain in a state of inner aspiration and calm, then gradually they lose their force and stop coming. So the consciousness is emptied of its lower movements.

But for instance, when undesirable thoughts come, if you look at them, observe them, if you take pleasure in following them in their movements, they will never stop coming. It is the same thing when you have undesirable feelings or sensations: if you pay attention to them, concentrate on them or even look at them with a certain indulgence, they will never stop. But if you absolutely refuse to receive and express them, after some time they stop. You must be patient and very persistent.

In a great aspiration, if you can put yourself into contact with something higher, some influence of your psychic being or some light from above, and if you can manage to put this in touch with these lower movements, naturally they stop more quickly. But before even being able to draw these things by aspiration, you can already stop those movements from finding expression in you by a very persistent and patient refusal. When thoughts which you do not like come, if you just brush them away and do not pay them any attention at all, after some time they won't come any longer. But you must do this very persistently and regularly.

Begin from the Outside

All forces upon earth tend towards expressing themselves. These forces come with the object of manifesting themselves and if you place a barrier and refuse expression, they may try to beat against the barrier for a time, but in the end, they will tire themselves out and not being manifested, they will withdraw and leave you quiet.

So you must never say: "I shall first purify my thought, purify

my body, purify my vital and then later I shall purify my action."
That is the normal order, but it never succeeds. The effective
order is to begin from the outside: "The very first thing is that I do
not do it, and afterwards, I desire it no longer and next I close my
doors completely to all impulses: they no longer exist for me, I am
now outside all that." This is the true order, the order that is
effective. First, not to do it. And then you will no longer desire and
after that it will go out of your consciousness completely.

Inner Cleanliness

I have known people (many, not only a few, I mean among those
who do yoga), I have known many who, every time they had a fine
aspiration, and their aspiration was very strong and they received
an answer to this aspiration, every time, the very same day or at
the latest the next day, they had a complete setback of consciousness and were facing the exact opposite of their aspiration. Such
things happen almost constantly. Well, these people have developed only the positive side. They make a kind of discipline of
aspiration, they ask for help, they try to come into contact with
higher forces, they succeed in this, they have experiences; but they
have completely neglected cleaning their room; it has remained as
dirty as ever, and so, naturally, when the experience has gone, this
dirt becomes still more repulsive than before.

One must never neglect to clean one's room, it is very important; inner cleanliness is at least as important as outer cleanliness.

Vivekananda has written (I don't know the original, I have only
read the French translation): "One must every morning clean
one's soul and one's body, but if you don't have time for both, it is
better to clean the soul than clean the body."

Blaming Oneself

Is blaming oneself a good method of progressing?

Blaming oneself? No, not necessarily. It may be useful, it is indeed useful from time to time in order to get out of the illusion of one's own perfection. But one wastes much energy in self-criticism. It is much better to use this same energy in making progress, a concrete progress, something more useful. For example, if you have thoughts which are unpleasant, ugly, vulgar and disturbing, and you say, "Ah, ah, how intolerable I am, I still have such thoughts, what a nuisance it is!", it would be much better to use this very energy simply to do this (*gesture*) and drive away the thoughts.

And this is only the first step. The second is to try to have other thoughts, to take interest in something else: either read or reflect, but in any case try to fill your mind with something more interesting, to use your energy in constructing rather than in destroying.

It is of course necessary from time to time to recognise one's faults; it is altogether indispensable. But to dwell too much upon them is not necessary. What is necessary is to use all one's energy in order to build up the qualities one wants to have and do what one wants to do. This is much more important.

Guard against Despair

For some people events are always contrary to what they desire or aspire for or believe to be good for them. They often despair. Is this a necessity for their progress?

Despair is never a necessity for progress, it is always a sign of weakness and *tamas*; it often indicates the presence of an adverse force, that is to say, a force that is purposely acting against sadhana.

So, in all circumstances of life you must always be very careful to guard against despair. Besides, this habit of being sombre, morose, of despairing, does not truly depend on events, but on a lack of faith in the nature. One who has faith, even if only in himself, can face all difficulties, all circumstances, even the most adverse, without discouragement or despair. He fights like a man to the end. Natures that lack faith also lack endurance and courage.

One Chooses to Be Weak

Mother, there are mistakes... one knows they are mistakes, but still it is as though one were pushed into making them. Then?

Pushed by what? Ah, this is exactly what happens! It is the lower nature, the instincts of the subconscient which govern you and make you do things you should not do. And so it is a choice between your will and accepting submission. There is always a moment when one can decide. . . .

And it is a choice between weak submission and a controlling will. And if the will is clear, if it is based on truth, if truly it obeys the truth and is clear, it always has the power to refuse the wrong movement. It is an excuse you give yourself when you say, "I could not." It is not true. It is that truly you have not wanted it in the right way. For there is always the choice between saying "yes" and saying "no". But one chooses to be weak and later gives oneself this excuse, saying, "It is not my fault; it was stronger than I." It is your fault if the thing was stronger than you. Because you are not these impulses, you are a conscious soul and an intelligent will, and your duty is to see that *this* is what governs you and not the impulses from below.

To Fall Back into Error

To fall back into an error which one *knows* to be an error, to make a mistake once again which one *knows* to be a mistake, this seems to me fantastic! It is a long time – well, at least relatively, by human reckoning – it is a long time I have been on earth, and I have yet not been able to understand that. It seems to me – it seems to me impossible. Wrong thoughts, wrong impulses, inner and outer falsehood, things which are ugly, base, so long as one does them or has them through ignorance – ignorance is there in the world – one understands, one is in the habit of doing them; it is ignorance, one does not know that it ought to be otherwise. But the moment the knowledge is there, the light is there, the moment one has seen the thing as it is, how can one do it again? That I do not understand!

Then what is one made of? One is made of shreds? One is made of goodness knows what, of jelly?... It can't be explained. But is there no incentive, no will, nothing? Is there no inner dynamism?

Strengthen the Will

Mother, how can one strengthen one's will?

Oh, as one strengthens muscles, by a methodical exercise. You take one little thing, something you want to do or don't want to do. Begin with a small thing, not something very essential to the being, but a small detail. And then, if, for instance, it is something you are in the habit of doing, you insist on it with the same regularity, you see, either not to do it or to do it – you insist on it and compel yourself to do it as you compel yourself to lift a weight – it's the same thing. You make the same kind of effort, but it is more of an inner effort. And after having taken little things like this – things relatively easy, you know – after taking these and succeeding with them, you can unite with a greater force and try a more complicated experiment. And gradually, if you do this regularly, you will end up by acquiring an independent and very strong will.

How to Will Truly

To learn how to will is a very important thing. And to will truly, you must unify your being. In fact, to be a being, one must first unify oneself. If one is pulled by absolutely opposite tendencies, if one spends three-fourths of his life without being conscious of himself and the reasons why he does things, is one a real being? One does not exist. One is a mass of influences, movements, forces, actions, reactions, but one is not a being. One begins to become a being when he begins to have a will. And one can't have a will unless he is unified.

And when you have a will, you will be able to say, say to the Divine: "I want what You want." But not before that. Because in order to want what the Divine wants, you must have a will, otherwise you can will nothing at all. You would like to. You would like it very much. You would very much like to want what the Divine wants to do. You don't possess a will to give to Him and to put at His service.

OTHER PERSONS AND FORCES

Others Are a Mirror

When something in a person seems to you completely unacceptable or ridiculous – "What! He is like that, he behaves like that, he
says things like that, he does things like that" – you should say to
yourself, "Well, well, but perhaps I do the same thing without
being aware of it. I would do better to look into myself first before
criticising him, so as to make sure that I am not doing the very
same thing in a slightly different way." If you have the good sense
and intelligence to do this each time you are shocked by another
person's behaviour, you will realise that in life your relations with
others are like a mirror which is presented to you so that you can
see more easily and clearly the weaknesses you carry within you.

In a general and almost absolute way anything that shocks you
in other people is the very thing you carry in yourself in a more or
less veiled, more or less hidden form, though perhaps in a slightly
different guise which allows you to delude yourself. And what in
yourself seems inoffensive enough, becomes monstrous as soon as
you see it in others.

Try to experience this; it will greatly help you to change
yourselves. At the same time it will bring a sunny tolerance to your
relationships with others, the goodwill which comes from understanding, and it will very often put an end to these completely
useless quarrels.

Look upon everything with a benevolent smile. Take all the
things which irritate you as a lesson for yourself and your life will
be more peaceful and more effective as well, for a great percentage of your energy certainly goes to waste in the irritation you feel
when you do not find in others the perfection that you would like
to realise in yourself.

You stop short at the perfection that others should realise and
you are seldom conscious of the goal you should be pursuing
yourself. If you are conscious of it, well then, begin with the work

which is given to *you*, that is to say, realise what you have to do and do not concern yourself with what others do, because, after all, it is not your business. And the best way to the true attitude is simply to say, "All those around me, all the circumstances of my life, all the people near me, are a mirror held up to me by the Divine Consciousness to show me the progress I must make. Everything that shocks me in others means a work I have to do in myself."

And perhaps if one carried true perfection in oneself, one would discover it more often in others.

Insults: Remain Immobile

It is much more difficult to remain calm, immobile, unshakable before something very unpleasant – whether it be words or acts levelled against you – infinitely more difficult than to answer with the same violence.

Suppose someone insults you; if in the face of these insults, you can remain immobile (not only outwardly, I mean integrally), without being shaken or touched in any way: you are there like a force against which one can do nothing and you do not reply, you do not make a gesture, you do not say a word, all the insults thrown at you leave you absolutely untouched, within and without; you can keep your heart-beats absolutely quiet, you can keep the thoughts in your head quite immobile and calm without their being in the least disturbed, that is, your head does not answer immediately by similar vibrations and your nerves don't feel clenched with the need to return a few blows to relieve themselves; if you can be like that, you have a static power, and it is infinitely more powerful than if you had that kind of force which makes you answer insult by insult, blow by blow and agitation by agitation.

Be Good for the Sake of Being Good

You must not cherish the illusion that if you want to follow the
straight path, if you are modest, if you seek purity, if you are
disinterested, if you want to lead a solitary existence and have a
clear judgment, things will become easy.... It is quite the contrary!
When you begin to advance towards inner and outer perfection,
the difficulties start at the same time.

I have very often heard people saying, "Oh! now that I am
trying to be good, everybody seems to be bad to me!" But this is
precisely to teach you that one should not be good with an
interested motive, one should not be good so that others will be
good to you – one must be good for the sake of being good.

It is always the same lesson: one must do as well as one can, the
best one can, but without expecting a result, without doing it with
a view to the result. Just this attitude, to expect a reward for a good
action – to become good because one thinks that this will make life
easier – takes away all value from the good action.

You must be good for the love of goodness, you must be just for
the love of justice, you must be pure for the love of purity and you
must be disinterested for the love of disinterestedness; then you
are sure to advance on the way.

The Only Way Out

You see, in the present condition of the world, circumstances are
always difficult. The whole world is in a condition of strife,
conflict, between the forces of truth and light wanting to manifest
and the opposition of all that does not want to change, which
represents in the past what is fixed, hardened and refuses to go.
Naturally, each individual feels his own difficulties and is faced by
the same obstacles.

There is only one way for you. It is a total, complete and
unconditional surrender. What I mean by that is the giving up not
only of your actions, work, ambitions, but also of all your feelings,

in the sense that all that you do, all that you are, is exclusively for the Divine. So, you feel above the surrounding human reactions – not only above them but protected from them by the wall of the Divine's Grace. Once you have no more desires, no more attachments, once you have given up all necessity of receiving a reward from human beings, whoever they are – knowing that the only reward that is worth getting is the one that comes from the Supreme and that never fails – once you give up the attachment to all exterior beings and things, you at once feel in your heart this Presence, this Force, this Grace that is always with you.

And there is no other remedy. It's the only remedy, for *everybody* without exception. To all those who suffer, it is the same thing that has to be said: all suffering is the sign that the surrender is not total. Then, when you feel in you a "bang", like that, instead of saying, "Oh, this is bad" or "This circumstance is difficult," you say, "My surrender is not perfect." Then it's all right. And then you feel the Grace that helps you and leads you, and you go on. And one day you emerge into that peace that nothing can trouble. You answer to all the contrary forces, the contrary movements, the attacks, the misunderstandings, the bad wills, with the same smile that comes from full confidence in the Divine Grace. And that is the *only* way out, there is none else. This world is a world of conflict, suffering, difficulty, strain; it is made of it. It has not yet changed, it will take some time before changing. And for each one there is a possibility of getting out. If you lean back on the presence of the Supreme Grace, that is the *only* way out.

. . .Don't expect human appreciation – because human beings don't know on what grounds to appreciate something, and, moreover, when there is something that is superior to them, they don't like it.

But where to get such a strength?

Within you. The Divine Presence is in you. It is in you. You look for it outside; look inside. It is in you. The Presence is there. You want the appreciation of others to get strength – you will never get it. The strength is in you. If you want, you can aspire for what seems to you the supreme goal, supreme light, supreme knowledge, supreme love. But it is in you – otherwise you would never be able to contact it. If you go deep enough inside you, you will find it there, like a flame that is always burning straight up.

And don't believe that it is so difficult to do. It is because the look is always turned outside that you don't feel the Presence. But if, instead of looking outside for support, you concentrate and you pray – inside, to the supreme knowledge – to know at each moment what is to be done, the way to do it, and if you give all you are, all you do in order to acquire perfection, you will feel that the support is there, always guiding, showing the way. And if there is a difficulty, then instead of wanting to fight, you hand it over, hand it over to the supreme wisdom to deal with it – to deal with all the bad wills, all the misunderstandings, all the bad reactions. If you surrender completely, it is no more your concern: it's the concern of the Supreme who takes it up and knows better than anybody else what is to be done. The only way out, only way out. There, my child.

Escape from Other Influences

Sweet Mother, how can we escape from other people's influence?

By concentrating more and more totally and completely on the Divine. If you aspire with all your ardour, if you want to receive only the divine influence, if all the time you pull back towards yourself what is taken, caught by other influences and with your will put it under the divine influence, you succeed in doing it. It's a work that can't be done in a day, in a minute; you must be vigilant for a very long time, for years; but one can succeed.

First of all you must will it.

For all things, first you must understand, will, and then begin to practise – begin by just a very little.

Open Only to the Divine

Sweet Mother, what does "an exclusive self-opening to the divine Power" mean?

Instead of self-opening we could put receptivity, something that opens in order to receive. Now, instead of opening and receiving from all sides and from everyone, as is usually done, one opens only to the Divine to receive only the divine force. It is the very opposite of what men usually do. They are always open on the surface, they receive all the influences from all sides. And then this produces inside them what we might call a *pot-pourri* (*Mother laughs*) of all kinds of contradictory movements which naturally create countless difficulties. So here, you are advised to open only to the Divine and to receive only the divine force to the exclusion of everything else. This diminishes all difficulties almost entirely.

Stepping Back

Most of you live on the surface of your being, exposed to the touch of external influences. You live almost projected, as it were, outside your own body, and when you meet some unpleasant being similarly projected you get upset. The whole trouble arises out of your not being accustomed to stepping back. You must always step back into yourself – learn to go deep within – step back and you will be safe. Do not lend yourself to the superficial forces which move in the outside world. Even if you are in a hurry to do something, step back for a while and you will discover to your surprise how much sooner and with what greater success your work can be done. If someone is angry with you, do not be caught in his vibrations but simply step back and his anger, finding no support or response, will vanish. Always keep your peace, resist all temptation to lose it. Never decide anything without stepping back, never speak a word without stepping back, never throw yourself into action without stepping back. All that belongs to the ordinary world is impermanent and fugitive, so there is nothing in it worth getting upset about. What is lasting, eternal, immortal and infinite – that indeed is worth having, worth conquering, worth possessing. It is Divine Light, Divine Love, Divine Life – it is also Supreme Peace, Perfect Joy and All-Mastery upon earth with the Complete Manifestation as the crowning. When you get the sense of the relativity of things, then whatever happens you can step back and look; you can remain quiet and call on the Divine Force and wait for an answer. Then you will know exactly what to do. Remember, therefore, that you cannot receive the answer before you are very peaceful. Practise that inner peace, make at least a small beginning and go on in your practice until it becomes a habit with you.

Attacks from Adverse Forces

Attacks from adverse forces are inevitable: you have to take them as tests on your way and go courageously through the ordeal. The struggle may be hard, but when you come out of it, you have gained something, you have advanced a step. There is even a necessity for the existence of the hostile forces. They make your determination stronger, your aspiration clearer.

It is true, however, that they exist because you gave them reason to exist. So long as there is something in you which answers to them, their intervention is perfectly legitimate. If nothing in you responded, if they had no hold upon any part of your nature, they would retire and leave you. In any case, they need not stop or hamper your spiritual progress. . . .

In any case, when an attack comes the wisest attitude is to consider that it comes from outside and to say, "This is not myself and I will have nothing to do with it." You have to deal in the same way with all lower impulses and desires and all doubts and questionings in the mind. If you identify yourself with them, the difficulty in fighting them becomes all the greater; for then you have the feeling that you are facing the never easy task of overcoming your own nature. But once you are able to say, "No, this is not myself, I will have nothing to do with it", it becomes much easier to disperse them.

Attack by an Adverse Force

The most important thing to do when you are attacked by an adverse force, is to say to yourself: "Yes, the force comes from outside and the attack is there, but there must certainly be a correspondence in my nature, otherwise it could not have attacked me. Well, I am going to look and find within me what allows this force to come and I am going to send it back or transform it or put the light of consciousness upon it so that it may be converted, or drive it away so that it remains no longer within me...." There is a way, isn't there? When the force comes, the adverse force, when it attacks, the part which corresponds rushes out to meet it, it goes forward. A kind of meeting takes place. If at that time, instead of being altogether overwhelmed or taken by surprise and off your guard, you observe very closely what it was within you that vibrated (it makes the sound tat, tat, tat: another thing has entered), then you can catch it. At that moment, you catch it and say to it: "Get out with your friends, I don't want you any longer!" You send away the two together, the part that attracted and the thing it attracted; they are sent away and you are absolutely clear.

The Hole Made by Boasting

In their relation with human beings [the hostile forces] take a very wicked pleasure in testing them. For example, if you are not extremely strong and extremely sincere, and you tell yourself, "Oh, I am sure of my faith" – this for instance among many other things – immediately something happens which is going to try to shake your faith completely. This is one... I suppose that's their diversion, their amusement.

How many times, you know, when someone boasts... it may be very childishly... but when someone boasts about something: "Oh, I am sure of that, I shall never make that mistake", immediately I see a hostile formation passing there, like that, and it enters by the little hole made by the boasting. It enters within, like that, and then penetrates, and so prepares everything for you to do exactly what you didn't want to. But this is an amusement, it is certainly not to help you to progress. (*Mother laughs*) But if you know how to take it, it does help you to progress. You say, "Good, another time I won't boast."

COURAGE, ENDURANCE, EFFORT

Fear is an Impurity

Fear is an impurity, one of the greatest impurities, one of those which come most directly from the anti-divine forces which want to destroy the divine action on earth; and the first duty of those who really want to do yoga is to eliminate from their consciousness, with all the might, all the sincerity, all the endurance of which they are capable, even the shadow of a fear. To walk on the path, one must be dauntless, and never indulge in that petty, small, feeble, nasty shrinking back upon oneself, which is fear.

An indomitable courage, a perfect sincerity and a sincere self-giving, so that one does not calculate or bargain, does not give with the idea of receiving, does not trust with the idea of being protected, does not have a faith which asks for proofs – it is this that is indispensable in order to walk on the path, and it is this alone which can truly shelter you from all danger.

Fear: A Lack of Trust

Why does one feel afraid?

I suppose it is because one is egoistic.

There are three reasons. First, an excessive concern about one's security. Next, what one does not know always gives an uneasy feeling which is translated in the consciousness by fear. And above all, one doesn't have the habit of a spontaneous trust in the Divine. If you look into things sufficiently deeply, this is the true reason. There are people who do not even know that That exists, but one could tell them in other words, "You have no faith in your destiny" or "You know nothing about Grace" – anything whatever, you may put it as you like, but the root of the matter is a lack of trust. If one always had the feeling that it is the best that happens in all circumstances, one would not be afraid.

Conquering Fear

One of the great remedies for conquering fear is to face boldly what one fears. You are put face to face with the danger you fear and you fear it no longer. The fear disappears. From the yogic point of view, the point of view of discipline, this is the cure recommended. In the ancient initiations, especially in Egypt, in order to practise occultism, as I was telling you last time, it was necessary to abolish the fear of death completely. Well, one of the practices of those days was to lay the neophyte in a sarcophagus and leave him in there for a few days, as though he were dead. Naturally, he was not left to die, neither of hunger nor suffocation, but still he remained lying there as though he were dead. It seems that cures you of all fear.

When fear comes, if one succeeds in putting upon it consciousness, knowledge, force, light, one can cure it altogether.

True Courage

True courage, in its deepest sense, is to be able to face everything, everything in life, from the smallest to the greatest things, from material things to those of the spirit, without a shudder, without physically... without the heart beginning to beat faster, without the nerves trembling or the slightest emotion in any part of the being. Face everything with a constant consciousness of the divine Presence, with a total self-giving to the Divine, and the whole being unified in this will; then one can go forward in life, can face anything whatever. I say, without a shudder, without a vibration; this, you know, is the result of a long effort, unless one is born with a special grace, born like that. But this indeed is still more rare.

Pleasure and Pain

If one can face suffering with courage, endurance, an unshakable faith in the divine Grace, if one can, instead of shunning suffering when it comes, enter into it with this will, this aspiration to go through it and find the luminous truth, the unvarying delight which is at the core of all things, the door of pain is often more direct, more immediate than that of satisfaction or contentment.

I am not speaking of pleasure because pleasure turns its back constantly and almost completely on this profound divine Delight.

Pleasure is a deceptive and perverse disguise which turns us away from our goal and we certainly should not seek it if we are eager to find the truth. Pleasure vapourises us; it deceives us, leads us astray. Pain brings us back to a deeper truth by obliging us to concentrate in order to be able to bear it, be able to face this thing that crushes us. It is in pain that one most easily finds the true strength again, when one is strong. It is in pain that one most easily finds the true faith again, the faith in something which is above and beyond all pain.

The Reason for Blows

"O Thou that lovest, strike! If Thou strike me not now, I shall know that Thou lovest me not."

Sri Aurobindo, Thoughts and Aphorisms

All who aspire for the divine perfection know that the blows which the Lord deals us in His infinite love and grace are the surest and quickest way to make us progress. And the harder the blows the more they feel the greatness of the divine Love.

Ordinary men, on the contrary, always ask God to give them an easy, pleasant and successful life. In every personal satisfaction they see a sign of divine mercy; but if on the contrary they meet with unhappiness and misfortune in life, they complain and say to God, "You do not love me."

In opposition to this crude and ignorant attitude, Sri Aurobindo says to the divine Beloved, "Strike, strike hard, let me feel the intensity of Thy love for me."

Many Blows Are Needed

Mother, even when one tries to think that one is powerless, there is something which believes one is powerful. So?

Ah, yes, ah, yes! Ah, it is very difficult to be sincere.... That is why the blows multiply and sometimes become terrible, because that's the only thing which breaks your stupidity. This is the justification of calamities. Only when you are in an acutely painful situation and indeed before something that affects you deeply, then that makes the stupidity melt away a little. But as you say, even when there is something that melts, there is still a little something which remains inside. And that is why it lasts so long...

How many blows are needed in life for one to know to the very depths that one is *nothing*, that one can do *nothing*, that one *does not exist*, that one is *nothing*, that there is no entity without the divine Consciousness and the Grace. From the moment one knows it, it is over; all the difficulties have gone. When one knows it integrally and there is nothing which resists... but till that moment... And it takes very long.

Never Get Discouraged

You must tell yourself, "With the means of transport at my disposal I have reached a certain point, but these means do not allow me to go further. What should I do?... Sit there and not stir any longer? – not at all. I must find other means of transport." This will happen quite often, but after a while you will get used to it. You must sit down for a moment, meditate, and then find other means. You must increase your concentration, your aspiration and your trust and with the new help which comes to you, make a new programme, work out other means to replace those you have left behind. This is how one progresses stage by stage.

But you must take great care to apply at each stage, as perfectly as possible, what you have gained or learnt. If you remain in an indrawn state of consciousness and do not apply materially the inner progress, a time will certainly come when you will not be able to move at all, for your outer being, unchanged, will be like a fetter pulling you back and hindering you from advancing. So, the most important point (what everybody says but only a few do) is to put into practice what you know. With that you have a good chance of succeeding, and with perseverance you will certainly get there.

You must never get discouraged when you find yourself before a wall, never say, "Oh! what shall I do? It is still there." In this way the difficulty will still be there and still there and still there, till the very end. It is only when you reach the goal that everything will suddenly crumble down.

If One Has Endurance

People have a beautiful experience and say, "Ah, now this is it!..." And then it settles down, diminishes, gets veiled, and suddenly something quite unexpected, absolutely commonplace and apparently completely uninteresting comes before you and blocks your way. And then you say, "Ah! what's the good of having made this progress if it's going to start all over again? Why should I do it? I made an effort, I succeeded, achieved something, and now it's as if I had done nothing! It's indeed hopeless." For you have no endurance.

If one has endurance, one says, "It's all right. Good, I shall begin again as often as necessary; a thousand times, ten thousand times, a hundred thousand times if necessary, I shall begin again – but I shall go to the end and nothing will have the power to stop me on the way."

This is most necessary. Most necessary.

Pay the Price

All of you who have come here have been told many things; you
have been put into contact with a world of truth, you live within it,
the air you breathe is full of it; and yet how few of you know that
these truths are valuable only if they are put into practice, and that
it is useless to talk of consciousness, knowledge, equality of soul,
universality, infinity, eternity, supreme truth, the divine presence
and... of all sorts of things like that, if you make no effort
yourselves to *live* these things and feel them concretely within you.
And don't tell yourselves, "Oh, I have been here so many years!
Oh, I would very much like to have the result of my efforts!" You
must know that very persistent efforts, a very steadfast endurance
are necessary to master the least weakness, the least pettiness, the
least meanness in one's nature. What is the use of talking about
divine Love if one can't love without egoism? What is the use of
talking about immortality if one is stubbornly attached to the past
and the present and if one doesn't want to give anything in order to
receive everything?

You are still very young, but you must learn *right away* that to
reach the goal you must know how to pay the price, and that to
understand the supreme truths you must put them into practice in
your daily life.

Effort Gives Joy

*An aim gives a meaning, a purpose to life, and this purpose
implies an effort; and it is in effort that one finds joy.*

Exactly. It is the effort which gives joy; a human being who does
not know how to make an effort will never find joy. Those who are
essentially lazy will never find joy – they do not have the strength
to be joyful! It is effort which gives joy. Effort makes the being
vibrate at a certain degree of tension which makes it possible for
you to feel the joy. . . .

It is only effort, in whatever domain it be – material effort, moral effort, intellectual effort – which creates in the being certain vibrations which enable you to get connected with universal vibrations; and it is this which gives joy. It is effort which pulls you out of inertia; it is effort which makes you receptive to the universal forces. And the one thing above all which spontaneously gives joy, even to those who do not practise yoga, who have no spiritual aspiration, who lead quite an ordinary life, is the exchange of forces with universal forces. People do not know this, they would not be able to tell you that it is due to this, but so it is.

RECEPTIVITY AND ASPIRATION

The Universal Vital Force

Sweet Mother, how can one draw on "the universal vital Force"?

One can do it in many ways.

First of all, you must know that it exists and that one can enter into contact with it. Secondly, you must try to make this contact, to feel it circulating everywhere, through everything, in all persons and all circumstances; to have this experience, for example, when you are in the countryside among trees, to see it circulating in the whole of Nature, in trees and things, and then commune with it, feel yourself close to it, and each time you want to deal with it, recall that impression you had and try to enter into contact.

Some people discover that with certain movements, certain gestures, certain activities, they enter into contact more closely. I knew people who gesticulated while walking... this truly gave them the impression that they were in contact – certain gestures they made while walking. But children do this spontaneously: when they give themselves completely in their games, running, playing, jumping, shouting; when they spend all their energies like that, they give themselves entirely, and in the joy of playing and moving and running they put themselves in contact with this universal vital force; they don't know it, but they spend their vital force in a contact with the universal vital force and that is why they can run without really feeling very tired, except after a very long time. . . .

I knew young people who had always lived in cities – in a city and in those little rooms one has in the big cities in which everyone is huddled. Now, they had come to spend their holidays in the countryside, in the south of France, and there the sun is hot. . . . When they walked around the countryside the first few days they really began to get a terrible headache and to feel absolutely uneasy because of the sun; but they suddenly thought: "Why, if we make friends with the sun it won't harm us any more!" And they began to make a kind of inner effort of friendship and trust in the sun, and when they were out in the sun, instead of trying to bend double and tell themselves, "Oh! how hot it is, how it burns!", they said, "Oh, how full of force and joy and love the sun is!" etc., they opened themselves like this (*gesture*), and not only did they not suffer any longer but they felt so strong afterwards that they went round telling everyone who said "It is hot" – telling them "Do as we do, you will see how good it is." And they could remain for hours in the full sun, bare-headed and without feeling any discomfort. It is the same principle.

It is the same principle. They linked themselves to the universal vital force which is in the sun and received this force which took away all that was unpleasant to them.

When one is in the countryside, when one walks under the trees and feels so close to Nature, to the trees, the sky, all the leaves, all the branches, all the herbs, when one feels a great friendship with these things and breathes that air which is so good, perfumed with all the plants, then one opens oneself, and by opening oneself communes with the universal forces. And for all things it is like that.

Receptivity to the Universal Vital Forces

Sweet Mother, do the universal vital forces have any limits?

I don't think that forces have a limit, because in comparison with us they are certainly unlimited. But it's our capacity of reception that is limited. We cannot absorb them beyond a certain measure, and then we must keep a balance between the expenditure and the capacity to receive. If one spends suddenly in a kind of impulse – for example, in an impulsive movement – if one spends much more than one has received, one needs a brief moment of concentration, calm, receptivity to absorb universal forces. You must put yourself in a certain condition to receive them; and then, they last for a certain time, and once you have spent them you must begin again to receive them. It is in this sense that there are limits. It isn't the forces that are limited, it is the receptivity.

*

How can we increase the receptivity? By progressing.

One must first know how to open himself and then, in a great quietude know how to assimilate the forces one has received, not to throw them out again. One must know how to assimilate them.

So the progress lies in a normal but progressive equilibrium, periods of assimilation – reception, assimilation – and periods of expenditure, and knowing how to balance the two, and alternate them in a rhythm which is your personal one. You must not go beyond your capacity, you must not remain below it, because the universal vital forces are not something which you could put into a strong box. They must circulate. So you must know how to receive and at the same time to spend, but to increase the capacity of reception so as to have more and more of the things which are to be used up, to be spent.

Three Sources of Vital Force

In the immense majority of people all their vital force comes to them from below, from the earth, from food, from all the sensations. From food... they draw vital energy out of food, and they... it is by seeing, hearing, touching, feeling that they contact the energies contained in matter. They draw them in this way. This is their customary food.

Now, some people have a very developed vital which they have subjected to a discipline – and they have a sense of immensity and are in contact with the world and the movements of world-forces. And so they can receive... if in a movement of calling... they can receive the universal vital forces which enter them and renew the dose of energy they need.

There are others, very rare ones – or maybe in very rare moments of their individual life – who have an aspiration for the higher consciousness, higher force, higher knowledge, and who, by this call, draw to themselves the forces of higher domains. And so this also renews in them very special energies, of a special value.

But unless one is practising yoga, a regular discipline, usually one does not often contact this source; one draws from the same level or from below.

Activity and Passivity in Sadhana

An active movement is one in which you throw your force out, that is, when something comes out from you – in a movement, a thought, a feeling – something which goes out from you to others or into the world. Passivity is when you remain just yourself like this, open, and receive what comes from outside. It does not at all depend on whether one moves or sits still. It is not that at all. To be active is to throw out the consciousness or force or movement from within outwards. To be passive is to remain immobile and receive what comes from outside. . . . "Activity in aspiration", that means that your aspiration goes out from you and rises to the Divine – in the tapasya, the discipline you undertake and when there are forces contrary to your sadhana you reject them. This is a movement of activity.

Now, if you want to get true inspiration, inner guidance, the guide, and if you want to have the force, to receive the force which will guide you and make you act as you should, then you do not move any longer, that is – I don't mean not move physically but nothing must come out from you any more and, on the contrary, you remain as though you were quite still, but open, and wait for the Force to enter, and then open yourself as wide as possible to take in all that comes into you. And it is this movement: instead of out-going vibrations there is a kind of calm quietude, but completely open, as though you were opening all your pores in this way to the force which must descend into you and transform your action and consciousness.

Receptivity is the result of a fine passivity.

The Flame and the Vase

You can be at once in the state of aspiration, of willing, which calls
down something – exactly the will to open oneself and receive, and
the aspiration which calls down the force you want to receive – and
at the same time be in that state of complete inner stillness which
allows full penetration, for it is in this immobility that one can be
penetrated, that one becomes permeable by the Force. Well, the
two can be simultaneous without the one disturbing the other, or
can alternate so closely that they can hardly be distinguished. But
one can be like that, like a great flame rising in aspiration, and at
the same time as though this flame formed a vase, a large vase,
opening and receiving all that comes down.

And the two can go together. And when one succeeds in having
the two together, one can have them constantly, whatever one
may be doing. Only there may be a slight, very slight displacement
of consciousness, almost imperceptible, which becomes aware of
the flame first and then of the vase of receptivity – of what seeks to
be filled and the flame that rises to call down what must fill the vase
– a very slight pendular movement and so close that it gives the
impression that one has the two at the same time.

Aspiration and Receptivity

Aspiration in everyone, no matter who it is, has the same power.
But the effect of this aspiration is different. For aspiration is
aspiration: if you have aspiration, in itself it has a power. Only,
this aspiration calls down an answer, and this answer, the effect,
which is the result of the aspiration, depends upon each one, for it
depends upon his receptivity. I know many people of this kind:
they say, "Oh! but I aspire all the time and still I receive nothing."
It is impossible that they should receive nothing, in the sense that
the answer is sure to come. But it is they who do not receive. The
answer comes but they are not receptive, so they receive
nothing. . . .

When you have an aspiration, a very active aspiration, your aspiration is going to do its work. It is going to call down the answer to what you aspire for. But if, later, you begin to think of something else or are not attentive or receptive, you do not even notice that your aspiration has received an answer. This happens very frequently. So people tell you: "I aspire and I don't receive anything, I get no answer!" Yes, you do have an answer but you are not aware of it, because you continue to be active in this way, like a mill turning all the time.

Find that Something

We can, simply by a sincere aspiration, open a sealed door in us and find... that Something which will change the whole significance of life, reply to all our questions, solve all our problems and lead us to the perfection we aspire for without knowing it, to that Reality which *alone* can satisfy us and give us lasting joy, equilibrium, strength, life.

All this you have heard many a time.

You have heard it – Oh! there are even some here who are so used to it that for them it seems to be the same thing as drinking a glass of water or opening a window to let in the sunlight. . . .

We have tried a little, but now we are going to try seriously!

The starting-point: to want it, truly want it, to need it. The next step: to think, *above all*, of that. A day comes, very quickly, when one is unable to think of anything else.

That is the one thing which counts. And then...

One formulates one's aspiration, lets the true prayer spring up from one's heart, the prayer which expresses the sincerity of the need. And then... well, one will see what happens.

Something will happen. Surely something will happen. For each one it will take a different form.

Aspiration is Like an Arrow

Aspiration is like an arrow, like this (*gesture*). So you aspire, want *very* earnestly to understand, know, enter into the truth. Yes? And then with that aspiration you do this (*gesture*). Your aspiration rises, rises, rises, rises straight up, very strong and then it strikes against a kind of... how to put it? ...lid which is there, hard like iron and extremely thick, and it does not pass through. And then you say, "See, what's the use of aspiring? It brings nothing at all. I meet with something hard and cannot pass!" But you know about the drop of water which falls on the rock, it ends up by making a chasm: it cuts the rock from top to bottom. Your aspiration is a drop of water which, instead of falling, rises. So, by dint of rising, it beats, beats, beats, and one day it makes a hole, by dint of rising; and when it makes the hole suddenly it springs out from this lid and enters an immensity of light, and you say, "Ah, now I understand."

It's like that.

So one must be very persistent, very stubborn and have an aspiration which rises straight upwards, that is, which does not go roaming around here and there, seeking all kinds of things.

Only this: to understand, understand, understand, to learn to know, to be.

When one reaches the very top, there is nothing more to understand, nothing more to learn, one *is*, and it's when one *is* that one understands and knows.

CONCENTRATION, MEDITATION, WORK

Concentrating the Attention

Whatever you may want to do in life, one thing is absolutely indispensable and at the basis of *everything*, the capacity of concentrating the attention. If you are able to gather together the rays of attention and consciousness on one point and can maintain this concentration with a persistent will, *nothing* can resist it – whatever it may be, from the most material physical development to the highest spiritual one. But this discipline must be followed in a constant and, it may be said, imperturbable way; not that you should always be concentrated on the same thing – that's not what I mean, I mean learning to concentrate.

And materially, for studies, sports, all physical or mental development, it is absolutely indispensable. And the value of an individual is proportionate to the value of his attention.

And from the spiritual point of view it is still more important. There is *no* spiritual obstacle which can resist a penetrating power of concentration. For instance, the discovery of the psychic being, union with the inner Divine, opening to the higher spheres, *all* can be obtained by an intense and obstinate power of concentration – but one must learn how to do it.

There is nothing in the human or even in the superhuman field, to which the power of concentration is not the key.

You can be the best athlete, you can be the best student, you can be an artistic, literary or scientific genius, you can be the greatest saint with that faculty. And everyone has in himself a tiny little beginning of it – it is given to everybody, but people do not cultivate it.

Concentration

What is concentration?

It is to bring back all the scattered threads of consciousness to a single point, a single idea. Those who can attain perfect attention succeed in everything they undertake; they will always make a rapid progress. And this kind of concentration can be developed exactly like the muscles; one may follow different systems, different methods of training. Today we know that the most pitiful weakling, for example, can with discipline become as strong as anyone else. One should not have a will which flickers out like a candle.

The will, the concentration must be cultivated; it is a question of method, of regular exercise. If you will, you can.

But the thought "What's the use?" must not come in to weaken the will. The idea that one is born with a certain character and can do nothing about it is a stupidity.

Concentrate in the Centre of Aspiration

It is always better to try to concentrate in a centre, the centre of aspiration, one might say, the place where the flame of aspiration burns, to gather in all the energies there, at the solar plexus centre and, if possible, to obtain an attentive silence as though one wanted to listen to something extremely subtle, something that demands a complete attention, a complete concentration and total silence. And then not to move at all. Not to think, not to stir, and make that movement of opening so as to receive all that can be received, but taking good care not to try to know what is happening while it is happening, for if one wants to understand or even to observe actively, it keeps up a sort of cerebral activity which is unfavourable to the fullness of the receptivity – to be silent, as totally silent as possible, in an attentive concentration, and then be still.

If one succeeds in this, then, when everything is over, when one comes out of meditation, some time later – usually not immediately – from within the being something new emerges in the consciousness: a new understanding, a new appreciation of things, a new attitude in life – in short, a new way of being.

Dynamic Meditation

I think the most important thing is to know why one meditates; this is what gives the quality of the meditation and makes it of one order or another.

You may meditate to open yourself to the divine Force, you may meditate to reject the ordinary consciousness, you may meditate to enter the depths of your being, you may meditate to learn how to give yourself integrally; you may meditate for all kinds of things. You may meditate to enter into peace and calm and silence – this is what people generally do, but without much success. But you may also meditate to receive the Force of transformation, to discover the points to be transformed, to trace out the line of progress. And then you may also meditate for very practical reasons: when you have a difficulty to clear up, a solution to find, when you want help in some action or other. You may meditate for that too.

I think everyone has his own mode of meditation. But if one wants the meditation to be dynamic, one must have an aspiration for progress and the meditation must be done to help and fulfil this aspiration for progress. Then it becomes dynamic.

Meditation and Progress

The number of hours spent in meditation is no proof of spiritual progress. It is a proof of your progress when you no longer have to make an effort to meditate. Then you have rather to make an effort to stop meditating: it becomes difficult to stop meditation,

difficult to stop thinking of the Divine, difficult to come down to
the ordinary consciousness. Then you are sure of progress, then
you have made real progress when concentration in the Divine is
the necessity of your life, when you cannot do without it, when it
continues naturally from morning to night whatever you may be
engaged in doing. Whether you sit down to meditation or go about
and do things and work, what is required of you is consciousness; that is the one need – to be constantly conscious of the
Divine.

> *But is not sitting down to meditation an indispensable discipline,*
> *and does it not give a more intense and concentrated union with*
> *the Divine?*

That may be. But a discipline in itself is not what we are seeking.
What we are seeking is to be concentrated on the Divine in all that
we do, at all times, in all our acts and in every movement. There
are some here who have been told to meditate; but also there are
others who have not been asked to do any meditation at all. But it
must not be thought that they are not progressing. They too follow
a discipline, but it is of another nature. To work, to act with
devotion and an inner consecration is also a spiritual discipline.
The final aim is to be in constant union with the Divine, not only in
meditation but in all circumstances and in all the active life.

Meditate under All Circumstances

You may be engaged in the most active action, for example, in
playing basketball, which needs a great deal of movement, and yet
not lose the attitude of inner meditation and concentration upon
the Divine. And when you get that, you will see that all you do
changes its quality; not only will you do it better, but you will do it
with an altogether unexpected strength, and at the same time keep
your consciousness so high and so pure that nothing will be able to
touch you any longer. And note that this can go so far that even if

an accident occurs, it will not hurt you. Naturally, this is a peak, but it is a peak to which one can aspire.

Do not fall into the very common error of believing that you must sit in an absolutely quiet corner where nobody passes by, where you are in a classical position and altogether immobile, in order to be able to meditate – it is not true. What is needed is to succeed in meditating under all circumstances, and I call "meditating" not emptying your head but concentrating yourself in a contemplation of the Divine; and if you keep this contemplation within you, all that you do will change its quality – not its appearance, for apparently it will be the same thing, but its quality. And life will change its quality, and you, you will feel a little different from what you were, with a peace, a certitude, an inner calm, an unchanging force, something which never gives way.

Control of the Body

Those who despise physical activities are people who won't be able to take a single step on the true path of integral yoga, unless they first get rid of their contempt. Control of the body in all its forms is an indispensable basis. A body which dominates you is an enemy, it is a disorder you cannot accept. It is the enlightened will in the mind which should govern the body, and not the body which should impose its law on the mind. When one knows that a thing is bad, one must be capable of not doing it. When one wants something to be realised, one must be able to do it and not be stopped at every step by the body's inability or ill-will or lack of collaboration; and for that one must follow a physical discipline and become master in one's own home.

It is very fine to escape into meditation and from the height of one's so-called grandeur look down on material things, but one who is not master in his own home is a slave.

The Body Needs Activity

The body needs activity: if you keep it inactive, it will begin to revolt by becoming sick and so on. It needs an activity, it really needs an activity like planting flowers, building a house, something really material. You must feel it. Some people do exercises, some ride bicycles, there are countless activities, but in your little group you must all come to an agreement so that each one can find the activity which suits his temperament, his nature and his need. But not with ideas. Ideas are not much good, ideas give you preconceptions, for example, "That is a good work, that work is not worthy of me," and all that sort of nonsense. There is no bad work – there are only bad workers. All work is good when you know how to do it in the right way. Everything. And it is a kind of communion. If you are fortunate enough to be conscious of an inner light, you will see that in your manual work, it is as if you called the Divine down into things; then the communion becomes very concrete, there is a whole world to be discovered, it is marvellous.

"Remember and Offer"

When we are concentrated in mental movements or intellectual pursuits, why do we sometimes forget or lose touch with the Divine?

You lose it because your consciousness is still divided. The Divine has not settled into your mind; you are not wholly consecrated to the Divine Life. Otherwise you could concentrate to any extent upon such things and still you would have the sense of being helped and supported by the Divine.

In all pursuits, intellectual or active, your one motto should be, "Remember and Offer." Let whatever you do be done as an offering to the Divine. And this too will be an excellent discipline for you; it will prevent you from doing many foolish and useless things.

THE DIVINE WORK

The Three Victories

The first victory is to create an individuality. And then later, the second victory is to give this individuality to the Divine. And the third victory is that the Divine changes your individuality into a divine being.

There are three stages: the first is to become an individual; the second is to consecrate the individual, that he may surrender entirely to the Divine and be identified with Him; and the third is that the Divine takes possession of this individual and changes him into a being in His own image, that is, he too becomes divine.

Generally, all the yogas stopped at the second. When one had succeeded in surrendering the individual and giving him without reserve to the Divine to be identified with Him, one considered that his work was finished, that all was accomplished.

But *we* begin there, and we say, "No, this is only a beginning. We want this Divine with whom we are identified to enter our individuality and make it into a divine personality acting in a divine world. And this is what we call transformation. But the other precedes it, must precede it. If that is not done, there is no possibility of doing the third. One can't go from the first to the third; one must pass through the second.

Come for the Divine Work

Each time someone comes to tell me, "I come for *my* yoga", I say, "Oh, no! then don't come. It is much more difficult here than anywhere else."...

If someone comes to tell me, "I come to work, I come to make myself useful", it is all right. But if someone comes and says, "I have many difficulties outside, I can't manage to overcome these difficulties, I want to come here because it will help me", I say,

"No, no, it will be *much* more difficult here; your difficulties will increase *considerably*." And that is what it means, because they are no longer isolated difficulties; they are collective difficulties.

So in addition to your own personal difficulty you have all the frictions, all the contacts, all the reactions, all the things which come from outside. As a test. Exactly on the weak point, the thing that's most difficult to solve; it is there that you will hear from someone the phrase which was just the one you did not want to hear; someone will make towards you that gesture which was exactly the one which could shock you; you find yourself facing a circumstance, a movement, a fact, an object, anything at all – just the things which... "Ah, how I should have liked this not to happen!" And it's that which will happen. And more and more. Because you do not do your yoga for yourself alone. You do the yoga for everybody – without wanting to – automatically.

So when people come and tell me, "I come here for peace, quietness, leisure, to do my yoga", I say, "No, no, no! go away immediately somewhere else, you will be much more peaceful anywhere else than here."

If someone comes and says, "Well, here I am, I feel that I should consecrate myself to the divine Work, I am ready to do any work at all that you give me", then I say, "Good, that's all right. If you have goodwill, endurance, and some capacity, it is all right. But to find the solitude necessary for your inner development it is better to go somewhere else, *anywhere else*, but not here."

Why This Divine Work?

All this perfection which we are going to acquire is not for a personal and selfish end, it is in order to be able to manifest the Divine, it is put at the service of the Divine. We do not pursue this development with a selfish intention of personal perfection; we pursue it because the divine Work has to be accomplished.

But why do we do this divine Work? It is to make ourselves...

No, not at all! It is because that's the divine Will. It is not at all for a personal reason, it must not be that. It is because it's the divine Will and it's the divine Work.

So long as a personal aspiration or desire, a selfish will, get mingled in it, it always creates a mixture and is not exactly an expression of the divine Will. The only thing which must count is the Divine, His Will, His manifestation, His expression. One is here for that, one is that, and nothing else. And so long as there is a feeling of self, of the ego, the person, which enters, well, this proves that one is not yet what one ought to be, that's all. I don't say that this can be done overnight but still this indeed is the truth.

True Integrity

Mother, why is it that here, in work, some people venture to satisfy their fancies and thus much money is wasted?

It is not money alone that is wasted!

Energy, Consciousness is *infinitely*, a thousand times more wasted than money. Should there be no wastage... my word, I believe the Ashram couldn't be here! There is not a second when there isn't any wastage – sometimes it is worse than that. There is this habit – hardly conscious, I hope - of absorbing as much Energy, as much Consciousness as one can and using it for one's personal satisfactions. That indeed is something which is happening every minute. If all the Energy, all the Consciousness which is constantly poured out upon you all, were used for the true purpose, that is, for the divine work and the preparation for the divine work, we should be already very far on the road, much farther than we are. But everybody, more or less consciously, and in any case instinctively, absorbs as much Consciousness and Energy as he can and as soon as he feels this Energy in himself, he uses it for his personal ends, his own satisfaction.

Who thinks that all this Force that is here, that is infinitely greater, infinitely more precious than all money-forces, this Force which is here and is given consciously, constantly, with an endless perseverance and patience, only for *one sole purpose*, that of realising the divine work – who thinks of not wasting it? Who realises that it is a sacred duty to make progress, to prepare oneself to understand better and live better? For people live *by* the divine Energy, they live *by* the divine Consciousness, and use them for their personal, selfish ends.

You are shocked when a few thousand rupees are wasted but not shocked when there are... when streams of Consciousness and Energy are diverted from their true purpose!

If one wants to do a divine work upon earth, one must come with tons of patience and endurance. One must know how to live in eternity and wait for the consciousness to awaken in everyone – the consciousness of what *true* integrity is.

Doing the Divine Work

Mother, if for instance in the long jump one makes an effort to jump a greater and greater distance, how does one do the divine work?

Eh? Excuse me, it is not for the pleasure of doing the long jump, it is to make your body more perfect in its functioning, and, therefore, a more suitable instrument for receiving the divine forces and manifesting them.

Why, everything, everything one does in this place must be done in this spirit, otherwise you do not even profit by the opportunity given to you, the circumstances given to you. I explained to you the other day, didn't I? that the Consciousness is here, penetrating all things and trying to manifest in all movements. But if you, on your side, tell yourself that the effort you are making, the progress you are making, you make in order to become more capable of receiving this Consciousness and of manifesting it, the work will naturally be much better and much quicker.

PEACE AND QUIET

The Illusion of Action

Agitation, haste, restlessness lead nowhere. It is foam on the sea; it is a great fuss that stops with itself. Men have a feeling that if they are not all the time running about and bursting into fits of feverish activity, they are doing nothing. It is an illusion to think that all these so-called movements change things. It is merely taking a cup and beating the water in it; the water is moved about, but it is not changed for all your beating. This illusion of action is one of the greatest illusions of human nature. It hurts progress because it brings on you the necessity of rushing always into some excited movement. If you could only perceive the illusion and see how useless it all is, how it changes nothing! Nowhere can you achieve anything by it. Those who are thus rushing about are the tools of forces that make them dance for their own amusement. And they are not forces of the best quality either.

Whatever has been done in the world has been done by the very few who can stand outside the action in silence; for it is they who are the instruments of the Divine Power. They are dynamic agents, conscious instruments; they bring down the forces that change the world. Things can be done in that way, not by a restless activity. In peace, in silence and in quietness the world was built; and each time that something is to be truly built, it is in peace and silence and quietness that it must be done. It is ignorance to believe that you must run from morning to night and labour at all sorts of futile things in order to do something for the world.

Learn to be Quiet

The noise made by all the words, all the ideas in your head is so deafening that it prevents you from hearing the truth when it wants to manifest.

To learn to be quiet and silent... When you have a problem to solve, instead of turning over in your head all the possibilities, all the consequences, all the possible things one should or should not do, if you remain quiet with an aspiration for goodwill, if possible a need for goodwill, the solution comes very quickly. And as you are silent you are able to hear it.

When you are caught in a difficulty, try this method: instead of becoming agitated, turning over all the ideas and actively seeking solutions, of worrying, fretting, running here and there inside your head – I don't mean externally, for externally you probably have enough common sense not to do that! but inside, in your head – *remain quiet*. And according to your nature, with ardour or peace, with intensity or widening or with all these together, implore the Light and wait for it to come.

In this way the path would be considerably shortened.

"Peace, Peace, Peace"

How can we establish a settled peace and silence in the mind?

First of all, you must want it.

And then you must try and must persevere, continue trying. . . . You sit quietly, to begin with; and then, instead of thinking of fifty things, you begin saying to yourself, "Peace, peace, peace, peace, peace, calm, peace!" You imagine peace and calm. You aspire, ask that it may come: "Peace, peace, calm." And then, when something comes and touches you and acts, say quietly, like this, "Peace, peace, peace." Do not look at the thoughts, do not listen to the thoughts, you understand. You must not pay attention to everything that comes. You know, when someone bothers you a great deal and you want to get rid of him, you don't listen to him, do you? Good! You turn your head away (*gesture*) and think of something else. Well, you must do that: when thoughts come, you must not look at them, must not listen to them, must not pay any attention at all, you must behave as though they did not exist, you see! And then, repeat all the time like a kind of – how shall I put it? – as an idiot does, who repeats the same thing always. Well, you must do the same thing; you must repeat, "Peace, peace, peace." So you try this for a few minutes and then do what you have to do; and then, another time, you begin again; sit down again and then try. Do this on getting up in the morning, do this in the evening when going to bed. You can do this… look, if you want to digest your food properly, you can do this a few minutes before eating. You can't imagine how much this helps your digestion! Before beginning to eat you sit quietly for a while and say, "Peace, peace, peace! and *everything* becomes calm (*Mother stretches out her arms on both sides*) and then you must continue; and there comes a time when you no longer need to sit down, and no matter what you are doing, no matter what you are saying, it is always "Peace, peace, peace." Everything remains here, like this, it does not enter (*gesture in front of the forehead*), it remains like this. And then one is always in a perfect peace… after some years.

But at the beginning, a very small beginning, two or three minutes, it is very simple. For something complicated you must make an effort, and when one makes an effort one is not quiet. It is difficult to make an effort while remaining quiet. Very simple, very simple, you must be very simple in these things. It is as though you were learning how to call a friend: by dint of being called he comes. Well, make peace and calm your friends and call them: "Come, peace, peace, peace, peace, come!"

Sit Down Quietly

When you have a little time, whether it is one hour or a few minutes, tell yourself, "At last, I have some time to concentrate, to collect myself, to relive the purpose of my life, to offer myself to the True and the Eternal." If you took care to do this each time you are not harassed by outer circumstances, you would find out that you were advancing very quickly on the path. Instead of wasting your time in chattering, in doing useless things, reading things that lower the consciousness. . . it is better to be moderate, balanced, patient, quiet, but never to lose an opportunity that is given to you, that is to say, to utilise for the true purpose the unoccupied moment before you.

When you have nothing to do, you become restless, you run about, you meet friends, you take a walk, to speak only of the best; I am not referring to things that are obviously not to be done. Instead of that, sit down quietly before the sky, before the sea or under trees, whatever is possible (here you have all of them) and try to realise one of these things – to understand why you live, to learn how you must live, to ponder over what you want to do and what should be done, what is the best way of escaping from the ignorance and falsehood and pain in which you live.

Make Your Consciousness Vast

Sweet Mother, how can we make our consciousness vast?

Vast? Ah, there are many ways of doing this.

The easiest way is to identify yourself with something vast. For instance, when you feel that you are shut up in a completely narrow and limited thought, will, consciousness, when you feel as though you were in a shell, then if you begin thinking about something very vast, as for example, the immensity of the waters of an ocean, and if really you can think of this ocean and how it stretches out far, far, far, far, in all directions, like this (*Mother stretches out her arms*), how, compared with you it is so far, so far that you cannot see the other shore, you cannot reach its end anywhere, neither behind or in front nor to the right or left... it is wide, wide, wide, wide... you think of this and then you feel that you are floating on this sea, like that, and that there are *no* limits.... This is very easy. Then you can widen your consciousness a little.

Other people, for example, begin looking at the sky; and then they imagine all those spaces between all those stars, and all... that kind of infinity of spaces in which the earth is a tiny point, and you too are just a very tiny point, smaller than an ant, on the earth. And so you look at the sky and feel that you are floating in these infinite spaces between the planets, and that you are growing vaster and vaster to go farther and farther. Some people succeed with this.

There is a way also by trying to identify yourself with all things upon earth. For example, when you have a small narrow vision of something and are hurt by others' vision and point of view, you must begin by shifting your consciousness, try to put it in others, and try gradually to identify yourself with all the different ways of thinking of all others. This is a little more... how shall I put it?... dangerous. Because to identify oneself with the thought and will of others means to identify oneself with a heap of stupidities (*Mother laughs*) and bad wills, and this may bring consequences which are not very good. But still, some people do this more easily. For instance, when they are in disagreement with someone, in order to widen their consciousness they try to put themselves in the place of the other and see the thing not from their own point of view but from the point of view of the other. This widens the consciousness, though not as much as by the first ways I spoke about, which are quite innocent. They don't do you any harm, they do you much good. They make you very peaceful.

Open to the Higher Regions

If you open to the higher regions of consciousness and the force descends from above, quite naturally it establishes a silence in the lower regions, for they are governed by this higher power which descends. This comes from higher regions of the mind or from beyond, even from the supermind. So when this force and consciousness come down and enter into the consciousness of a lower plane, this consciousness becomes naturally quiet, for it is as though invaded, flooded by that higher light which transforms it.

In fact, this is even the only way of establishing a constant silence in one's mind. It is to open oneself to higher regions and let this higher consciousness, force, light descend constantly into the lower mind and take possession of it. And here, when this happens, this lower mind can remain constantly quiet and silent, because it is this one which acts and fills the whole being. One can act, write and speak without the mind being active, with this force which comes from above penetrating the mind and using it; and the mind itself becomes just a passive instrument. And in fact, this is the only way of establishing silence; for once this is established, the silence is established, the mind does not stir any longer, it acts only under the impulsion of this force when it manifests in it. It is like a very quiet, very silent field and the force when it comes puts the elements into movement and uses them, and it finds expression through the mind without the mind being agitated. It remains very quiet.

THE SPIRIT AND THE PSYCHIC BEING

Spiritual Experience

You speak of spiritual experience. What is an experience and how can one have it?

It is something which puts you in contact with a consciousness higher than the one you usually have. You have a certain feeling about yourself, you are not even aware of it, it is for you your ordinary condition, you understand. Well, if suddenly you become conscious within of something very different and much higher, then, whatever it may be, this will be a spiritual experience. You may formulate it with a mental idea, you may not formulate it; you may explain it to yourself, you may not; it may last, it may not, it may be instantaneous. But when there is this essential difference in the consciousness and when, naturally, the quality that comes is very... much higher, clearer, purer than what one usually has, then one can call this a spiritual experience; this means that there are thousands of different things which can be called spiritual experiences.

Should we aspire to have a spiritual experience?

I think it is wiser to aspire to make progress or to be more conscious or to be better or do better than aspire for a spiritual experience; because that might open the door to more or less imaginary and falsified experiences, to movements of the vital which take on the appearance of higher things. One may deceive oneself by having an aspiration for experiences. In fact, the experience must come spontaneously, as the result of inner progress, but not for itself or in itself.

Come Out of Words

The main trouble is that you think with words, but these words are empty of meaning; most of the time they are mere words – you talk of the Divine, you talk of the Supreme, you talk of Yoga, you say many things, but does all that correspond in your head to something concrete? to a thought, a feeling, a clear idea, an experience? Or are they simply words?

. . . You must see the thing, the experience behind the words. Here we speak of "Yoga" but elsewhere one would speak differently; some would say, "I am seeking my *raison d'être*", and so on. Those who have a religious bent will say, "I want to find the divine Presence." There are fifty ways of saying the thing but it is the *thing* which is important; you must feel it in your head, in your heart, everywhere. It must be concrete, living, otherwise you cannot advance. You must come out of words and get into action – get into the experience, get into life.

Contacting "That"

There is "something", there is a reality which is beyond all our expressions, but which we can succeed in contacting by practising a discipline. We can identify ourselves with it. Once one is identified with it one knows what it is, but one cannot express it, for words cannot say it. So, if you use one kind of vocabulary, if you have a particular mental conviction, you will use the vocabulary corresponding to that conviction. If you belong to another group which has another way of speaking, you will call it or even think about it in that way. I am telling you this to give you the true impression, that there is something there which cannot be grasped – grasped by thought – but which exists. But the name you give it matters little, that's of no importance, it *exists*. And so the only thing to do is to enter into contact with it – not to give it a name or describe it. In fact, there is hardly any use giving it a name or describing it. One must try to enter into contact, to concentrate upon it, live it, live that reality, and whatever the name you give it is not at all important once you have the experience. The experience alone counts. And when people associate the experience with a particular expression – and in so narrow a way, so closed up in itself that apart from this formula one can find nothing – that is an inferiority. One must be able to *live* that reality through all possible paths, all occasions, all formations; one must live it, for that indeed is true, for that is supremely good, that is all-powerful, that knows all, that... Yes, one can live that, but one cannot speak about it. And if one does speak, all that one says about it has no great importance. It is only a way of speaking, that is all. There is an entire line of philosophers and people who have replaced the notion of God by the notion of an impersonal Absolute or by a notion of Truth or a notion of justice or even by a notion of progress – of something eternally progressive; but for one who has within him the capacity of identifying himself with that, what has been said about it hasn't much importance. Sometimes one may read a whole book of philosophy and not progress a step farther. Sometimes one may be quite a fervent devotee of a religion and not progress. There are people who have spent entire lifetimes seated in contemplation and attained nothing. There are people (we have well-known examples) who used to do the most modest of manual works, like a cobbler mending old shoes, and who had an experience. It is altogether beyond what one thinks and says of it. It is some gift that's there, that is all. And all that is needed is to be that – to succeed in identifying oneself with it and live it. At times you read one sentence in a book and that leads you there. Sometimes you read entire books of philosophy or religion and they get you nowhere. There are people, however, whom the reading of philosophy books helps to go ahead. But all these things are secondary. There is only one thing that's important: that is a sincere and persistent will, for these things don't happen in a twinkling. So one must persevere. When someone feels that he is not advancing, he must not get discouraged; he must try to find out what it is in the nature that is opposing, and then make the necessary progress. And suddenly one goes forward. And when you reach the end you have an experience. And what is remarkable is that people who have followed altogether different paths, with altogether different mental constructions, from the greatest believer to the most unbelieving, even materialists, have arrived at that experience, it is the same for everyone. Because it is true – because it is real, because it is the sole reality. And it is quite simply *that*. I do not say anything more. This is of no importance, the way one speaks about it, what is important is to follow the path, *your* path, no matter which – yes, to go there.

Birth into the Spirit

In the individual existence, [the spirit] is what makes all the difference; so long as one just speaks of the spirit and it is something one has read about, whose existence one vaguely knows about, but not a very concrete reality for the consciousness, this means that one is not born into the spirit. And when one is born into the spirit, it becomes something much more concrete, much more living, much more real, much more tangible than the whole material world. And this is what makes the essential difference between beings. When *that* becomes spontaneously real – the true, concrete existence, the atmosphere one can freely breathe – then one knows one has crossed over to the other side. But so long as it is something rather vague and hazy – you have heard about it, you know that it exists, but... it has no concrete reality – well, this means that the new birth has not yet taken place.

A Reversal of Consciousness

There is a moment – because it is a question which becomes more and more intense and more and more acute – when you have even the feeling, precisely, that things are strange, that is, they are not real; a moment comes when this sensation that you have of yourself, of being yourself, becomes strange, a kind of sense of unreality. And the question continues coming up: "But then, what is myself?" Well, there is a moment when it comes up with so much concentration and such intensity that with this intensity of concentration suddenly there occurs a reversal, and then, instead of being on this side you are on that side, and when you are on that side everything is very simple; you understand, you know, you are, you live, and then you see clearly the unreality of the rest, and this is enough.

You see, one may have to wait for days, months, years, centuries, lives, before this moment comes. But if one intensifies his aspiration, there is a moment when the pressure is so great and the intensity of the question so strong that something turns over in the consciousness, and then this is absolutely what one feels: instead of being here one is there, instead of seeing from outside and seeking to see within, one is inside; and the minute one is within, absolutely everything changes, completely, and all that seemed to him true, natural, normal, real, tangible, all that, immediately, – yes, it seems to him very grotesque, very queer, very unreal, quite absurd; but one has touched something which is supremely true and eternally beautiful, and this one never loses again.

Once the reversal has taken place, you can glide into an external consciousness, not lose the ordinary contact with the things of life, but that remains and it never moves. You may, in your dealings with others, fall back a little into their ignorance and blindness, but there is always something there, living, standing up within, which does not move any more, until it manages to penetrate everything, to the point where it is over, where the blindness disappears for ever. And this is an absolutely tangible experience, something more concrete than the most concrete object, more concrete than a blow on your head, something more real than anything whatever.

This is why I always say... when people ask me how one may know whether he is in contact with his psychic being or how one may know whether he has found the Divine, well, it makes me laugh; for when it happens to you it is over, you can no longer ask any questions, it is done; you do not ask how it happens, it is done.

Contact with One's Psychic Being

In the ordinary life there's not one person in a million who has a conscious contact with his psychic being, even momentarily. The psychic being may work from within, but so invisibly and unconsciously for the outer being that it is as though it did not exist. And in most cases, the immense majority, almost the totality of cases, it's as though it were asleep, not at all active, in a kind of torpor.

It is only with the sadhana and a very persistent effort that one succeeds in having a conscious contact with his psychic being. . . .

In almost, almost all cases, a very very sustained effort is needed to become aware of one's psychic being. Usually it is considered that if one can do it in thirty years one is very lucky – thirty years of sustained effort, I say. It may happen that it's quicker. But this is so rare that immediately one says, "This is not an ordinary human being." That's the case of people who have been considered more or less divine beings and who were great yogis, great initiates.

The Psychic Being

[The psychic being] is a centre of light and truth and knowledge and beauty and harmony which the Divine Self in each of you creates by his presence, little by little; it is influenced, formed and moved by the Divine Consciousness of which it is a part and parcel. It is in each of you the deep inner being which you have to find in order that you may come in contact with the Divine in you. It is the intermediary between the Divine Consciousness and your external consciousness; it is the builder of the inner life, it is that which manifests in the outer nature the order and rule of the Divine Will. If you become aware in your outer consciousness of the psychic being within you and unite with it, you can find the pure Eternal Consciousness and live in it; instead of being moved by the Ignorance as the human being constantly is, you grow aware of the presence of an eternal light and knowledge within you, and to it you surrender and are integrally consecrated to it and moved by it in all things.

For your psychic being is that part of you which is already given to the Divine. It is its influence gradually spreading from within towards the most outward and material boundaries of your consciousness that will bring about the transformation of your entire nature. There can be no obscurity here; it is the luminous part in you. Most people are unconscious of this psychic part within them; the effort of Yoga is to make you conscious of it, so that the process of your transformation, instead of a slow labour extending through centuries, can be pressed into one life or even a few years.

The psychic being is that which persists after death, because it is your eternal self; it is this that carries the consciousness forward from life to life.

The psychic being is the real individuality of the true and divine individual within you. For your individuality means your special mode of expression and your psychic being is a special aspect of the one Divine Consciousness that has taken shape in you.

The Temple within You

In the depths of your consciousness is the psychic being, the temple of the Divine within you. This is the centre round which should come about the unification of all these divergent parts, all these contradictory movements of your being. Once you have got the consciousness of the psychic being and its aspiration, these doubts and difficulties can be destroyed. It takes more or less time, but you will surely succeed in the end. Once you have turned to the Divine, saying, "I want to be yours", and the Divine has said, "Yes", the whole world cannot keep you from it. When the central being has made its surrender, the chief difficulty has disappeared. The outer being is like a crust. In ordinary people the crust is so hard and thick that they are not conscious of the Divine within them. If once, even for a moment only, the inner being has said, "I am here and I am yours", then it is as though a bridge has been built and little by little the crust becomes thinner and thinner until the two parts are wholly joined and the inner and the outer become one.

The Value of a Physical Body

This kind of work, this harmonisation and organisation of the being around the divine Centre can only be done in a physical body and on earth. That is truly the essential and original reason for physical life. For, as soon as you are no longer in a physical body, you can no longer do it *at all*.

And what is still more remarkable is that only human beings can do it, for only human beings have at their centre the divine Presence in the psychic being. . . .

And yet, human beings come into a physical body without knowing why, most of them go through life without knowing why, they leave their body without knowing why, and they have to begin the same thing all over again, indefinitely, until one day, someone comes along and tells them, "Be careful! you know, there is a purpose to this. You are here for this work, don't miss your opportunity!"

And how many years are wasted.

The Work of the Psychic Being

What is the work of the psychic being?

What is the work of the psychic being? You want it to have some work? What do you want to say exactly? What is its function? Ah! very well. One could put it this way, that it is like an electric wire that connects the generator with the lamp. Now, if someone has understood, let him explain what I said! . . .

The generator is the Divine and the lamp is the body.

It is the body, it is the visible being.

So, that is its function. This means that if there were no psychic in Matter, it would not be able to have any direct contact with the Divine. And it is happily due to this psychic presence in Matter that the contact between Matter and the Divine can be direct and all human beings can be told, "You carry the Divine within you, and you have only to enter within yourself and you will find Him."

Difficulties and the Psychic Being

I think the more psychic one is, usually, the more difficulties he has. Only, one is armed to face the difficulties. But the more psychic one is, the more is he in contradiction with the present state of the world. So when one is in opposition with something, the result is difficulties. And I have noticed that most often those who have many difficulties are those who are in a more or less close contact with their psychic being. If you want to speak about outer circumstances – I am not speaking of the character, that's quite different, but of outer circumstances – the people who have to struggle most and would have most reason to suffer are those who have a very developed psychic being.

First, the development of the psychic being has a double result which is concomitant. That is, with the development of the psychic being, the sensitivity of the being grows. And with the growth of sensitivity there is also the growth of the capacity for suffering; but there is the counterpart, that is, to the extent to which one is in relation with the psychic being, one faces the circumstances of life in an altogether different way and with a kind of inner freedom which makes one capable of withdrawing from a circumstance and not feeling the shock in the ordinary way. You can face the difficulty or outer things with calm, peace, and a sufficient inner knowledge not to be troubled. So, on one side you are more sensitive and on the other you have more strength to deal with the sensitivity.

The Psychic and the Truth

Does the psychic being identify itself with the inner Truth?

It organises itself around it and enters into contact with it. The psychic is moved by the Truth. The Truth is something eternally self-existent and dependent on nothing in time or space, whereas the psychic being is a being that grows, takes form, progresses, individualises itself more and more. In this way it becomes more and more capable of manifesting this Truth, the eternal Truth that is one and permanent. The psychic being is a progressive being, which means that the relation between the psychic being and the Truth is a progressive one. It is not possible to become aware of one's psychic being without becoming aware at the same time of the inner Truth. All those who have had this experience – not a mental experience but an integral experience of contact with the psychic being, not a contact with the idea they have constructed of it, but a truly concrete contact – all say the same thing: from the very minute this contact takes place, one is absolutely conscious of the eternal Truth within oneself and one sees that it is the purpose of life and the guide of the world.

The Knowledge of the Psychic

The perception of the exterior consciousness may deny the perception of the psychic. But the psychic has the true knowledge, an intuitive, instinctive knowledge. It says, "I know; I cannot give reasons, but I know." For its knowledge is not mental, based on experience or proved true. It does not believe after proofs are given: faith is the movement of the soul whose knowledge is spontaneous and direct. Even if the whole world denies and brings forward a thousand proofs to the contrary, still it knows by an inner knowledge, a direct perception that can stand against everything, a perception by identity. The knowledge of the psychic is something which is concrete and tangible, a solid mass. You can also bring it into your mental, your vital and your physical; and then you have an integral faith – a faith which can really move mountains.

Doing Yoga with the Head

I believe there is a vast difference between an effort for transformation which, precisely, comes from the psychic centre of the being and a kind of mental construction to obtain something.

I don't know, it is very difficult to make oneself understood, but so long as the thing goes on in the head in this way (*Mother turns a finger near her forehead*), it has no power. It has a very little force that is extremely limited. And all the time it belies itself. One thinks that with great difficulty one collects a will, artificial enough, besides, and one tries to catch something, and the very next minute it has all vanished. And one doesn't even realise it; one asks oneself, "How does it happen to turn out like that?"

I don't know, indeed it seems to me very difficult to do yoga with the head – unless one is gripped.

The will is not in the head.

The will – what I call the will – is something that's here (*Mother points to the centre of the chest*), which has a power of action, a power of realisation.

What one does exclusively in the head is subject to countless fluctuations; it is not possible to construct a theory, for instance, without there intervening immediately things which give all the opposite arguments. And so, there's the great skill of the mind, you know: it can prove no matter what, argue about anything at all. Consequently one does not go a step farther. Even if momentarily one catches an idea that has a certain force, unless one can keep that state of intensity, as soon as there is a relaxation all the contrary things come along, and all, as you know, with the charm of their expression. So it is a ceaseless battle.

The Heart Has Wings

There are people in whom the psychic movement, the emotional impulse is stronger than intellectual understanding. They feel an irresistible attraction for the Divine without knowing, without having the slightest idea of what it is, of what it can be, what it represents – nothing, no intellectual notion – but a kind of impulse, attraction, a need, an inevitable need.

And these people who have that, if, I may say as a result of the Grace, they have a mind which does not trouble them, does not question, does not discuss, go very fast. . . .

There are others who understand first, who are very intellectual, have studied, can play with words and ideas, who will give you brilliant lectures on all the philosophies, all the religions, all human conceptions and who, perhaps, will take years to advance one step. Because all that goes on in the head.

Many things go on in the head. I have told you this already several times, the head is like a public square. Anything at all can enter there, come, cross over, go out, and create a lot of disorder. And people who are in the habit of playing with ideas are the ones most hampered from going farther. It is a game that's pretty, attractive; it gives you the impression that you are not altogether ordinary, at the level of ordinary life, but it cuts the wings.

It's not the head which has wings: it's the heart.

THE EGO AND SELF-GIVING

Get Out of the Ego

The whole universe moves in accordance with [your] ego: you are at the centre, and the universe turns round you. If you look at yourself attentively, you will see it is like that. Your vision of the universe – that's you at the centre and the universe all around. So there is no place for anything else. It is not the universe you see: it is yourself you see in the universe.

So, at first, to begin with, one must be able to get out of the ego. Afterwards, it has to be, you understand, in a certain state of inexistence. Then you begin to perceive things as they are, from a little higher up. But if you want to know things as they really are, you must be *absolutely* like a mirror: silent, peaceful, immobile, impartial, without preferences and in a state of total receptivity. And if you are like that, you will begin to see that there are many things you are not aware of, but which are there, and which will start becoming active in you.

Then you will be able to be *in* these things instead of being exclusively enclosed within the little point you are in the universe.

There are all kinds of ways of getting out of yourself. But it is indispensable if you want to begin to know things as they are and not in terms of yourself.

The Hard Shell of Ego

This sense of one's own person becomes a kind of cage, a prison which shuts you in, prevents you from being true, from knowing truly, acting truly, understanding truly. It is as though someone had put you in a very hard shell and you were compelled to stay there.

This is the first sensation you have. Afterwards you begin to tap against the shell in order to break it. Sometimes it resists very long.

But still, when you begin to feel this, that what you believed to be yourself, the person doing things and for whom they are done, the person who exists and makes you what you are, yes, when you pass from this to the consciousness that this is a prison preventing you from being truly yourself, then you have made great progress, and there is hope. You feel yourself stifled, crushed, absolutely shut up in a prison without air, without light, without an opening, and then you begin pushing from inside, pushing, pushing, pushing so that it may break.

And the day it breaks, the day it opens, suddenly, you enter the psychic consciousness. And then you understand. And then, truly, if you have a sense of humour, you laugh; you realise your stupidity.

Cut the Knot of the Ego

Sweet Mother, what does the "knot of the ego" mean?

Knot? Oh! It is an image, you see. But it is something that clings to you and holds you as tightly as a well-made rope knot. And so it is always said that in order to progress truly the first thing to do is to cut the knot of the ego. It is very expressive and makes a good image, doesn't it? – one is tied up, one is shut up in oneself, bound as in a prison by knots which tie up all parts of the being together; it is this which produces a cohesion. But at the same time it is a limitation, a limiting. You cannot receive all the forces you would like to, because you are enclosed in this shell made of a heap of knots in the rope that's tying you.

Sweet Mother, how can we cut the knot of the ego?

How to cut it? Take a sword and strike it (*laughter*), when one becomes conscious of it. For usually one is not; we think it quite normal, what happens to us; and in fact it is very normal but we think it quite good also. So to begin with one must have a great clear-sightedness to become aware that one is enclosed in all these knots which hold one in bondage. And then, when one is aware that there's something altogether tightly closed in there – so tightly that one has tried in vain to move it – then one imagines his will to be a very sharp sword-blade, and with all one's force one strikes a blow on this knot (imaginary, of course, one doesn't take up a sword in fact), and this produces a result. Of course, you can do this work from the psychological point of view, discovering all the elements constituting this knot, the whole set of resistances, habits, preferences, of all that holds you narrowly closed in. So when you grow aware of this, you can concentrate and call the divine Force and the Grace and strike a good blow on this formation, these things so closely held, like that, that nothing can separate them. And at that moment you must resolve that you will no longer listen to these things, that you will listen only to the divine Consciousness and will do no other work except the divine work without worrying about personal results, free from all attachment, free from all preference, free from all wish for success, power, satisfaction, vanity, all this.... All this must disappear and you must see only the divine Will incarnated in your will and making you act. Then, in this way, you are cured.

The Ego and "Pulling"

What attitude should one take to get out of the ego?

Attitude? It is rather a will, isn't it? You must will it.... What should one do, are you asking that?

The surest means is to give oneself to the Divine; not to try to draw the Divine to oneself but try to give oneself to the Divine. Then you are compelled at least to come out a little from yourself to begin with. Usually, you know, when people think of the Divine, the first thing they do is to "pull" as much as they can into themselves. And then, generally, they receive nothing at all. They tell you, "Ah! I called, I prayed and I did not have the answer. I had no answer, nothing came." But then, if you ask, "Did you offer yourself?" – "No, I pulled." – "Ah, yes, that is why it did not come!" It is not that it did not come, it is that when you pull you remain so shut up in your ego, . . . it raises a wall between what is to be received and yourself. You put yourself in prison and then you are astonished that in your prison you feel nothing.

Prison, and still more, with no windows on the street. Throw yourself out (*Mother opens her hands*), give yourself without holding back anything, simply for the joy of giving yourself. Then there's a chance that you may feel something.

Never Try to Pull the Force

I would like to recommend something to you. In your desire for progress and your aspiration for realisation, take great care not to attempt to pull the forces towards you. Give yourself, open yourself with as much disinterestedness as you can attain through a constant self-forgetfulness, increase your receptivity to the utmost, but *never* try to *pull* the Force towards you, for wanting to pull is already a dangerous egoism. You may aspire, you may open yourself, you may give yourself, but never seek to take. When things go wrong, people blame the Force, but it is not the Force that is responsible: it is ambition, egoism, ignorance and the weakness of the vessel.

Give yourself generously and with a perfect disinterestedness and from the deeper point of view nothing bad will ever happen to you. Try to take and you will be on the brink of the abyss.

Give Instead of Taking

If one were spread out in all things, if all the vibrations which come and go expressed the need to merge into everything, to widen oneself, grow, not by remaining within one's limits but coming out of them, and finally to be identified with everything, one would no longer have anything to lose for one would have everything. Only, one doesn't know this. And so, as one doesn't know, one can't do it. One tries to take, accumulate, accumulate, accumulate, but that is impossible, one can't accumulate. One must identify oneself. And then, the little bit one gives, one wants to get back: one gives a good thought, one expects some recognition; one gives a little affection, one expects it from others... for one doesn't have the ability to become the good thought in everything, one doesn't have the ability to be the affection, the tender love in all things. One feels just like that, all cut up and limited, and fears to lose everything, fears to lose what one has because one would be impoverished. On the other hand, if one were able to identify oneself, one would no longer need to pull. The more one spreads out, the more one has. The more one gets identified, the more one becomes. And then, instead of taking, one gives. And the more one gives, the more one grows.

Give Everything

The more you give yourself to the Divine the more He is with you, totally, constantly, at every minute, in all your thoughts, all your needs, and there is no aspiration which does not receive an immediate answer; and you have the sense of a complete, constant intimacy, of a total nearness. It is as though you carried... as though the Divine were all the time with you; you walk and He walks with you, you sleep and He sleeps with you, you eat and He eats with you, you think and He thinks with you, you love and He is the love you have. But for this one must give himself entirely, totally, exclusively, reserve nothing, keep nothing for himself and not keep back anything, not disperse anything also: the least little thing in your being which is not given to the Divine is a waste; it is the wasting of your joy, something that lessens your happiness by that much, and all that you don't give to the Divine is as though you were holding it in the way of the possibility of the Divine's giving Himself to you. You don't feel Him close to yourself,

constantly with you, because you don't belong to Him, because
you belong to hundreds of other things and people; in your
thought, your action, your feelings, impulses... there are millions
of things which you do not give Him, and that is why you don't feel
Him always with you, because all these things are so many screens
and walls between Him and you. But if you give Him everything, if
you keep back nothing, He will be constantly and totally with you
in all that you do, in all that you think, all that you feel, always, at
each moment. But for this you must give yourself absolutely, keep
back nothing; each little thing that you hold back is a stone you put
down to build up a wall between the Divine and yourself.

Make the Gift of Your Will

You can at every minute make the gift of your will in an aspiration
– and an aspiration which formulates itself very simply, not just
"Lord, Thy will be done", but "Grant that I may do as well as I can
the best thing to do."

You may not know at every moment what is the best thing to do
nor how to do it, but you can place your will at the disposal of the
Divine to do the best possible, the best thing possible. You will see
it will have marvellous results. Do this with consciousness,
sincerity and perseverance, and you will find yourself getting
along with gigantic strides. It is like that, isn't it? One must do
things with all the ardour of one's soul, with all the strength of
one's will; do at every moment the best possible, the best thing
possible. What others do is not your concern – this is something I
shall never be able to repeat to you often enough.

Offer Your Will

You have a will and you can offer that will. Take the example of
becoming conscious of your nights. If you take the attitude of
passive surrender, you would say, "When it is the Divine Will that

I should become conscious, then I shall become conscious." On the other hand, if you offer your will to the Divine, you begin to will, you say, "I will become conscious of my nights." You have the will that it should be done; you do not sit down idle and wait. The surrender comes in when you take the attitude that says, "I give my will to the Divine. I intensely want to become conscious of my nights, I have not the knowledge, let the Divine Will work it out for me." Your will must continue to act steadily, not in the way of choosing a particular action or demanding a particular object, but as an ardent aspiration concentrated upon the end to be achieved. This is the first step.

The Divine Will Is Unmistakable

How are we to know, you will ask, when it is the Divine Will that makes us act? The Divine Will is not difficult to recognise. It is unmistakable. You can know it without being very far on the path. Only you must listen to its voice, the small voice that is here in the heart. Once you are accustomed to listen, if you do anything that is contrary to the Divine Will, you feel an uneasiness. If you persist on the wrong track, you get very much disturbed. If, however, you give some material excuse as the cause of your uneasiness and proceed on your way, you gradually lose the faculty of perception and finally you may go on doing all kinds of wrong and feel no uneasiness. But if, when once you feel the least disturbance, you stop and ask of your inner self, "What is the cause of this?" then you do get the real answer and the whole thing becomes quite clear. Do not try to give a material excuse when you feel a little depression or a slight uneasiness. When you stop and look about for the reason, be absolutely straight and sincere. At first your mind will construct a very plausible and beautiful explanation. Do not accept it, but look beyond and ask, "What is it that is behind this movement? Why am I doing this?" Finally you will discover, hidden in a corner, the little ripple – a slight wrong turn or twist in your attitude that is causing the trouble or disturbance.

Knowing the Divine Will

There are four conditions for knowing the divine Will:
   The first essential condition: an absolute sincerity.
   Second: To overcome desires and preferences.
   Third: To silence the mind and listen.
   Fourth: To obey immediately when you receive the order.
If you persist you will perceive the divine Will more and more clearly. But even before you know what it is, you can make an offering of your own will and you will see that all circumstances will be so arranged as to make you do the right thing. But you must not be like that person I knew who used to say, "I always see the divine Will in others." That can land you anywhere, there is nothing more dangerous, for if you think you see the divine Will in others, you are sure to do their will, not the divine Will. There too we can say that not one among many, many human beings acts in accord with the divine Will.

You know the story of the irritable elephant, his mahout, and the man who would not make way for the elephant. Stanc ıg in the middle of the road, the man said to the mahout, "The divine Will is in me and the divine Will wants me not to move." The driver, a man of some wit, answered, "But the divine Will in the elephant wants you to move!"

The Right Attitude

There are some scrupulous people who set problems to themselves and find it very difficult to solve them, because they state the problem wrongly. I knew a young woman who was a theosophist and was trying to practise; she told me, "We are taught that the divine Will must prevail in all that we do, but in the morning when I have my breakfast, how can I know whether God wants me to put two lumps of sugar in my coffee or only one?"... And it was quite touching, you know, and I had some trouble explaining to her that the spirit in which she drank her coffee, the attitude she had towards her food, was much more important than the number of lumps of sugar she put into it.

It is the same with all the little things one does at every moment. The divine Consciousness does not work in the human way, It does not decide how many lumps of sugar you will put in your coffee. It gradually puts you in the right attitude towards actions, things – an attitude of consecration, suppleness, assent, aspiration, goodwill, plasticity, effort for progress – and this is what counts, much more than the small decision you take at every second. One may try to find out what is the truest thing to do, but it is not by a mental discussion or a mental problem that these things can be resolved. It is in fact by an inner attitude which *creates* an atmosphere of harmony – progressive harmony – in which all one does will necessarily be the best thing that could be done in those particular circumstances.

FAITH AND THE GRACE

Keep Faith

[We must have] faith that always what is for the best happens. We may for the moment not consider it as the best because we are ignorant and also blind, because we do not see the consequences of things and what will happen later. But we must keep the faith that if it is like that, if we rely on the Divine, if we give Him the full charge of ourselves, if we let Him decide everything for us, well, we must know that it is always what is best for us which happens. This is an absolute fact. To the extent to which you surrender, the best happens to you. This may not be in conformity with what you would like, your preference or desire, because these things are blind: it is the best from the spiritual point of view, the best for your progress, your development, your spiritual growth, your *true* life. It is always that. And you must keep this faith, because faith is the expression of a trust in the Divine and the full self-giving you make to the Divine. And when you make it, it is something absolutely marvellous. That's a fact, these are not just words, you understand, it is a fact. When you look back, all kinds of things which you did not understand when they happened to you, you realise as *just* the thing which was necessary in order to compel you to make the needed progress. *Always*, without exception. It is our blindness which prevents us from seeing it.

Faith through Aspiration

Can one have faith through aspiration?

What? Faith through aspiration? I think so, because it is rare to have it spontaneously, to be born with it. Very few people have this good luck to have a spontaneous faith. But if one is very sincere in one's aspiration, one gets it. Aspiration can bring everything, provided it is sincere and constant. One always has a tiny element of faith within oneself, whether it be faith in what one's parents have said or in the books one has studied. After all, all your education is based upon a faith of this kind. Those who have educated you have told you certain things. You had no means of checking, because you were too young and had no experience. But you have faith in what they told you and you go forward on that faith. So everyone has a tiny bit of faith, and to increase it one can use one's aspiration.

A Childlike Trust

What are the conditions in which there is a descent of faith?

The most important condition is an almost childlike trust, the candid trust of a child who is sure that it will come, who doesn't even ask himself about it; when he needs something he is sure that it is going to come. Well, it is this, this kind of trust – this indeed is the most important condition.

To aspire is indispensable. But some people aspire with such a conflict inside them between faith and absence of faith, trust and distrust, between the optimism which is sure of victory and a pessimism which asks itself when the catastrophe will come. Now if this is in the being, you may aspire but you don't get anything. And you say, "I aspired but didn't get anything." It is because you demolish your aspiration all the time by your lack of confidence.

. . . "What I need will be given to me; if I pray I shall have an answer; if I am in a difficulty and ask for help, the help will come – and not only will it come but it will manage everything." If the trust is there, spontaneous, candid, unquestioning, it works better than anything else, and the results are marvellous. It is with the contradictions and doubts of the mind that one spoils everything, with this kind of notion which comes when one is in difficulties: "Oh, it is impossible! I shall never manage it. And if it is going to be aggravated, if this condition I am in, which I don't want, is going to grow still worse, if I continue to slide down farther and farther, if, if, if, if..." like that, and one builds a wall between oneself and the force one wants to receive. The psychic being has this trust, has it wonderfully, without a shadow, without an argument, without a contradiction. And when it is like that, there is not a prayer which does not get an answer, no aspiration which is not realised.

Watching Over One's Faith

Certainly a personal effort is needed to preserve one's faith, to let it grow within. Later – much later – one day, looking back, we may see that everything that happened, even what seemed to us the worst, was a Divine Grace to make us advance on the way; and then we become aware that the personal effort too was a grace. But before reaching that point, one has to advance much, to struggle much, sometimes even to suffer a great deal.

To sit down in inert passivity and say, "If I am to have faith I shall have it, the Divine will give it to me", is an attitude of laziness, of unconsciousness and almost of bad-will.

For the inner flame to burn, one must feed it; one must watch over the fire, throw into it the fuel of all the errors one wants to get rid of, all that delays the progress, all that darkens the path. If one doesn't feed the fire, it smoulders under the ashes of one's unconsciousness and inertia, and then, not years but lives, centuries will pass before one reaches the goal.

One must watch over one's faith as one watches over the birth of something *infinitely* precious, and protect it very carefully from everything that can impair it.

In the ignorance and darkness of the beginning, faith is the most direct expression of the Divine Power which comes to fight and conquer.

The Extent of the Grace

No matter how great your faith and trust in the divine Grace, no matter how great your capacity to see it at work in all circumstances, at every moment, at every point in life, you will never succeed in understanding the marvellous immensity of Its Action, and the precision, the exactitude with which this Action is accomplished; you will never be able to grasp to what extent the Grace does everything, is behind everything, organises everything, conducts everything, so that the march forward to the divine realisation may be as swift, as complete, as total and harmonious as possible, considering the circumstances of the world.

As soon as you are in contact with It, there is not a second in time, not a point in space, which does not show you *dazzlingly* this perpetual work of the Grace, this constant intervention of the Grace.

And once you have seen this, you feel you are never equal to it, for you should never forget it, never have any fears, any anguish, any regrets, any recoils... or even suffering. If one were in union with this Grace, if one saw It everywhere, one would begin living a life of exultation, of all-power, of infinite happiness.

And that would be the best possible collaboration in the divine Work.

The Need for the Grace

What is the way to accept the Grace with gratitude?

Ah! First of all you must feel the need for it.

This is the most important point. It is to have a certain inner humility which makes you aware of your helplessness without the Grace, that truly, without it you are incomplete and powerless. This, to begin with, is the first thing.

. . . And then, if you become aware that it is only the Grace which can do [what you cannot do], that the situation in which you find yourself, from there the Grace alone can pull you out, can give you the solution and the strength to come out of it, then, quite naturally an intense aspiration awakes in you, a consciousness which is translated into an opening. If you call, aspire, and if you hope to get an answer, you will quite naturally open yourself to the Grace.

And later – you must pay great attention to this (*Mother puts her finger on her lips*) – the Grace will answer you, the Grace will pull you out of the trouble, the Grace will give you the solution to your problem or will help you to get out of your difficulty. But once you are free from trouble and have come out of your difficulty, don't forget that it is the Grace which pulled you out, and don't think it is yourself. For this, indeed, is the important point. Most people, as soon as the difficulty has gone, say, "After all, I pulled myself out of the difficulty quite well."

There you are. And then you lock and bolt the door, you see, and you cannot receive anything any more. You need once again some acute anguish, some terrible difficulty for this kind of inner stupidity to give way, and for you to realise once more that you can do nothing. Because it is only when you grow aware that you are powerless that you begin to be just a little open and plastic. But so long as you think that what you do depends on your own skill and your own capacity, truly, not only do you close one door, but, you know, you close lots of doors one upon another, and bolt them. You shut yourself up in a fortress and nothing can enter there. That is the great drawback: one forgets very quickly. Quite naturally one is satisfied with one's own capacity.

The Grace and the Sinner

How can [the Grace] come to the help of the sinner?

It doesn't help the sinner to be a sinner! It helps the sinner to give up his sin; that is to say, It does not push away the sinner, saying, "I won't do anything for you." It is there, always, even when he is sinning, to help him to come out of it, but not to continue in his sin.

There is a great difference between this and the idea that you are bad and so "I won't look after you, I shall throw you far away from me, and whatever is to happen to you will happen, I am not concerned about it." This is the common idea. One says, "God has rejected me", you know. It is not that. You may not be able to feel the Grace, but It will always be there, even with the worst of sinners, even with the worst of criminals, to help him to change, to be cured of his crime and sin if he wants to. It won't reject him, but It won't help him to do evil. It wouldn't be the Grace any longer.

Identify With the Grace

It is the divine Grace which makes you progress, and with the divine Grace you feel the divine Joy. But instead of identifying yourself with the Grace which makes you progress, you identify yourself with the ugly thing you want to get rid of; and so, naturally, you feel like it and suffer.

That is an experiment you can make if you are just a little conscious. There is something in you which you don't want, something bad – for one reason or another you don't want it, you want to pull it out – well, if you identify yourself ever so little with that thing, you feel the pain of the extraction; if, on the contrary, you identify yourself with the divine Force which comes to liberate you, you feel the joy of the divine Grace – and you experience the deep delight of the progress you have made.

And this is a sure sign for you, a sure indication of what you identify yourself with. If you are identified with the forces from below, you suffer; if you are identified with the forces from above, you are happy.

CONTROLLING ONE'S THOUGHTS

Bad Thoughts

Sri Aurobindo says that all that one thinks one is, one can, by the very fact of that thinking, become. This knowledge of the fact that *all* that one thinks one can be, is a very important key for the development of the being, and not only from the point of view of the possibilities of the being, but also from that of the control and choice of what one will be, of what one wants to be.

This makes us understand the necessity of not admitting into ourselves any thought which destroys aspiration or the creation of the truth of our being. It reveals the considerable importance of not allowing what one doesn't want to be or doesn't want to do to formulate itself into thought within the being. Because to think these things is already a beginning of their realisation. From every point of view it is bad to concentrate on what one doesn't want, on what one has to reject, what one refuses to be, for the very fact that the thought is there gives to things one wants to reject a sort of right of existence within oneself. This explains the considerable importance of not letting destructive suggestions, thoughts of ill-will, hatred, destruction enter; for merely to think of them is already to give them a power of realisation. Sri Aurobindo says that thought is not the cause of existence but an intermediary, the instrument which gives form to life, to creation, and the control of this instrument is of foremost importance if one wants disorder and all that is anti-divine to disappear from creation.

One must not admit bad thoughts into oneself under the pretext that they are merely thoughts. They are tools of execution. And one should not allow them to exist in oneself if one doesn't want them to do their work of destruction.

Unpleasant Thoughts

Mother, at times unpleasant thoughts come and disturb us. How can we get rid of them?

There are several methods. Generally – but it depends on people – generally, the easiest way is to think of something else. That is, to concentrate one's attention upon something that has nothing to do with that thought, has no connection with that thought, like reading or some work – generally something creative, some creative work. For instance, those who write, while they are writing (let us take simply a novelist), while he is writing, all other thoughts are gone, for he is concentrated on what he is doing. When he finishes writing, if he has no control, the other thoughts will return. But precisely when one is attacked by a thought, one can try to do some creative work; for example, the scientist could do some research work, a special study to discover something, something that is very absorbing; that is the easiest way. Naturally, those who have begun to control their thought can make a movement of rejection, push aside the thought as one would a physical object. But that is more difficult and asks for a much greater mastery. If one can manage it, it is more active, in the sense that if you reject that movement, that thought, if you chase it off effectively and constantly or almost repeatedly, finally it does not come any more. But in the other case, it can always return. That makes two methods.

The third means is to be able to bring down a sufficiently great light from above which will be the "denial" in the deeper sense; that is, if the thought which comes is something dark (and especially if it comes from the subconscient or inconscient and is sustained by instinct), if one can bring down from above the light of a true knowledge, a higher power, and put that light upon the thought, one can manage to dissolve it or enlighten or transform it – this is the supreme method. This is still a little more difficult. But it can be done, and if one does it, one is cured – not only does the thought not come back but the very cause is removed.

The first step is to think of something else (but in this way, you know, it will be indefinitely repeated); the second is to fight; and the third is to transform. When one has reached the third step, not only is one cured but one has made a permanent progress.

Concentrate on What You Want to Be

Lest you get discouraged by your own faults, the Dhammapada gives you this solacing image: the purest lily can spring out of a heap of rubbish by the wayside. That is to say, there is nothing so rotten that it cannot give birth to the purest realisation.

Whatever may be the past, whatever may be the faults committed, whatever the ignorance in which one might have lived, one carries deep within oneself the supreme purity which can translate itself into a wonderful realisation.

The whole point is to think of that, to concentrate on that and not to be concerned with all the difficulties and obstacles and hindrances.

Concentrate exclusively on what you want to be, forget as entirely as possible what you do not want to be.

Imagination

I say to you never be dejected and disappointed but let your imagination be always hopeful and joyously plastic to the stress of the higher Truth, so that the latter may find you full of the necessary formations to hold its creative light.

The imagination is like a knife which may be used for good or evil purposes. If you always dwell in the idea and feeling that you are going to be transformed, then you will help the process of the Yoga. If, on the contrary, you give in to dejection and bewail that you are not fit or that you are incapable of realisation, you poison your own being. It is just on account of this very important truth that I am so tirelessly insistent in telling you to let anything happen but, for heaven's sake, not to get depressed. Live rather in the constant hope and conviction that what we are doing will prove a success. In other words, let your imagination be moulded by your faith in Sri Aurobindo.

Imagination Opens the Path

What is the function, the use of the imagination?

If one knows how to use it, as I said, one can create for oneself his own inner and outer life; one can build his own existence with his imagination, if one knows how to use it and has a power. In fact it is an elementary way of creating, of forming things in the world. I have always felt that if one didn't have the capacity of imagination he would not make any progress. Your imagination always goes ahead of your life. When you think of yourself, usually you imagine what you want to be, don't you, and this goes ahead, then you follow, then it continues to go ahead and you follow. Imagination opens for you the path of realisation. People who are not imaginative – it is very difficult to make them move; they see just what is there before their nose, they feel just what they are moment by moment and they cannot go forward because they are clamped by the immediate thing.

The Atmosphere You Create

You carry with you, around you, in you, the atmosphere created by your actions, and if what you do is beautiful, good and harmonious, your atmosphere is beautiful, good and harmonious; on the other hand, if you live in a sordid selfishness, unscrupulous self-interest, ruthless bad will, that is what you will breathe every moment of your life and that means misery, constant uneasiness; it means ugliness that despairs of its own ugliness.

*

When you are good, when you are generous, noble, disinterested, kind, you create in you, around you, a particular atmosphere and this atmosphere is a sort of luminous release. You breathe, you blossom like a flower in the sun; there is no painful recoil on yourself, no bitterness, no revolt, no miseries. Spontaneously, naturally, the atmosphere becomes luminous and the air you breathe is full of happiness. And this is the air that you breathe, in your body and out of your body, in the waking state and in the state of sleep, in life and in the passage beyond life, outside earthly life until your new life.

Every wrong action produces on the consciousness the effect of a wind that withers, of a cold that freezes or of burning flames that consume.

Every good and kind deed brings light, restfulness, joy – the sunshine in which flowers bloom.

Create Your Own Atmosphere

Sweet Mother, here it is written: "A spiritual atmosphere is more important than outer conditions; if one can get that and also create one's own spiritual air to breathe in and live in it, that is the true condition of progress."[1] *How can one get that and also create one's true spiritual atmosphere?*

. . . It is by... precisely by inner discipline; you can create your atmosphere by controlling your thoughts, turning them exclusively towards the sadhana, controlling your actions, turning them exclusively towards the sadhana, abolishing all desires and all useless, external, ordinary activities, living a more intense inner life, and separating yourself from ordinary things, ordinary thoughts, ordinary reactions, ordinary actions; then you create a kind of atmosphere around you.

For example, instead of reading any odd thing and chatting and

1. Sri Aurobindo, *Bases of Yoga*.

doing anything whatever, if you read only what helps you to follow the path, if you act only in conformity with what can lead you to the divine realisation, if you aboiish in yourself all desires and impulses turned towards external things, if you calm your mental being, appease your vital being, if you shut yourself against suggestions coming from outside and become immune to the action of people surrounding you, you create *such* a spiritual atmosphere that nothing can touch it, and it *no longer* depends *at all* on circumstances or on whom you live with or on the conditions you live in, because you are enclosed in your own spiritual atmosphere. And that is how one obtains it: by turning one's attention *solely* to the spiritual life, by reading only what can help in the spiritual life, by doing only what leads you to the spiritual life, and so on. Then you create your own atmosphere. But naturally, if you open all the doors, listen to what people tell you, follow the advice of this one and the inspirations of that one, and are full of desires for outside things, you cannot create a spiritual atmosphere for yourself. You will have an ordinary atmosphere like everybody else.

DEVELOPING THE MIND AND SENSES

Do Many Different Things

*Sweet Mother, at school it is not possible to take many subjects.
We have to specialise.*

Yes, yes! I have heard that, especially from your teachers. I don't
agree. And I know it very well, this is being continuously repeated
to me: if anything is to be done properly, one must specialise. It is
the same thing for sports also. It is the same thing for everything in
life. It is said and repeated, and there are people who will prove it:
to do something well one must specialise. One must do that and
concentrate. If one wants to become a good philosopher, one must
learn only philosophy, if one wants to be a good chemist, one must
learn chemistry only. And if one wants to become a good
tennis-player, one must play only tennis. That's not what I think,
that is all I can say. My experience is different. I believe there are
general faculties and that it is much more important to acquire
these than to specialise – unless, naturally, it be like M. and Mme.
Curie who wanted to develop a certain science, find something
new, then of course they were compelled to concentrate on that
science. But still that was only till they had discovered it; once
they had found it, nothing stopped them from widening their
mind.

This is something I have heard from my very childhood, and I
believe our great grand-parents heard the same thing, and from all
time it has been preached that if you want to succeed in something
you must do only that. And as for me, I was scolded all the time
because I did many different things! And I was always told I would
never be good at anything. I studied, I did painting, I did music,
and besides was busy with other things still. And I was told my
music wouldn't be up to much, my painting wouldn't be worth-
while, and my studies would be quite incomplete. Probably it is
quite true, but still I have found that this had its advantages – those

very advantages I am speaking about, of widening, making supple one's mind and understanding.

Education and Freedom

You see, the great thing here is that the principle of education is a principle of freedom, and to put it briefly, the whole life is organised on the maximum possible freedom in movement; that is, the rules, regulations, restrictions are reduced absolutely to the minimum. If you compare this with the way in which parents usually educate their children, with a constant "Don't do this", "You can't do that", "Do this", "Go and do that", and, you know, orders and rules, there is a considerable difference.

In schools and colleges everywhere there are infinitely more strict rules than what we have here. So, as one doesn't impose on you the absolute condition of making progress, you make it when it pleases you, you don't when it doesn't, and then you take things as easy as you can. There are some – I do not say this absolutely – there are some who try, but they try spontaneously. Of course from the spiritual point of view this is infinitely more valuable. The progress you will make because you feel within yourself the need to make it, because it is an impulsion that pushes you forward spontaneously, and not because it is something imposed on you like a rule – this progress, from the spiritual point of view, is infinitely greater. All in you that tries to do things well, tries to do it spontaneously and sincerely; it is something that comes from within you, and not because you have been promised rewards if you do well and punishments if you do badly. Our system is not based on this.

It is possible that at a certain moment something comes along to give you the impression that your effort has been appreciated, but the effort was not made in view of that; that is, these promises are not made beforehand nor are they balanced by equivalent punishments. This is not the practice here. Usually things are such, arranged in such a way, that the satisfaction of having done well seems to be the best of rewards and one punishes himself when he does badly, in the sense that one feels miserable and unhappy and ill at ease, and this is indeed the most concrete punishment he has. And so, all these movements, from the point of view of the inner spiritual growth, have an infinitely greater value than when they are the result of an outer rule.

Mental Culture

You have a mental instrument with many possibilities, faculties, but they are latent and need a special education, a special training so that they can express the Light. It is certain that in ordinary life the brain is the seat of the outer expression of the mental consciousness; well, if this brain is not developed, if it is crude, there are innumerable things which cannot be expressed, because they do not have the instrument required to express themselves. It would be like a musical instrument with most of its notes missing, and that produces a rough approximation but not something precise.

Mental culture, intellectual education changes the constitution of your brain, enlarges it considerably, and as a result the expression becomes more complete and more precise.

It is not necessary if you want to escape from life and go into inexpressible heights, but it is indispensable if you want to express your experience in outer life.

Mother, you said that if one develops these faculties of analysis, deduction and all that too much, they become obstacles to spiritual experiences, no?

If they are not controlled, mastered, yes. But not necessarily. Not necessarily. It might make the control a little more difficult, for naturally it is more difficult to master an individualised being than a crude one – with a completer individualisation the ego becomes more crystallised and also self-satisfied, doesn't it?... But granting that this difficulty has been overcome, well, in a highly developed individuality the result is infinitely superior to the one obtained in a crude and uneducated nature. I am not saying that the process of transformation or rather of consecration is not more difficult but once it is achieved the result is far superior.

This may very well be compared with musical instruments, one of which has a certain number of notes and the other ten times as many. Well, it is perhaps easier to play an instrument of four or five notes but the music that could be played on a complete keyboard is obviously far superior!

One could even compare this to an orchestra much more than to a simple instrument. A human being, a fully developed human individuality is very much like one of those stupendous orchestras which has hundreds and hundreds of players. It is obviously very difficult to control and conduct them but the result can be marvellous.

Organise Your Life

Some. . . cannot keep a cupboard in order or a drawer in order. They may be in a room which looks very tidy and very neat outwardly, and then you open a drawer or a cupboard, it is like a battle-field! Everything is pell-mell. You find everything in a jumble; nothing is arranged. These are people with a poor little head in which ideas lie in the same state as their material objects. They have not organised their ideas. They haven't put them in order. They live in a cerebral confusion. And that is a sure sign, I have never met an exception to this rule: people who don't know how to keep their things in order – their ideas are in disorder in their heads, always. They exist together, the most contradictory ideas are put together, and not through a higher synthesis, don't you believe it: simply because of a disorder and an incapacity to organise their ideas. You don't need to speak even for ten minutes with people if you can manage to enter their room and open the drawers of their tables and look into their cupboard. You know in what state they are, don't you?

. . . One must organise one's own things – and at the same time one's own ideas – in the same way, and must know exactly where things are and be able to go straight to them, because one's organisation is logical. It is your own logic – it may not be your neighbour's logic, not necessarily, it is your own logic – but your organisation being logical, you know exactly where a thing is and, as I told you, if that thing is displaced, you know it immediately. And those who can do that are generally those who can put their ideas into order and can also organise their character and can finally control their movements. And then, if you make progress, you succeed in governing your physical life: you begin to have a control over your physical movements. If you take life in that way, truly it becomes interesting. If one lives in a confusion, a disorder, an inner and outer chaos in which everything is mixed up and one is conscious of nothing and still less is master of things, this is not living.

One's Own Way of Thinking

One needs years of very attentive, very careful, very reasonable, very coherent work, organisation, selection, construction, in order to succeed simply in forming, oh, simply this little thing, *one's own way of thinking*!

One believes he has his own way of thinking. Not at all. It depends totally upon the people one speaks with or the books he has read or on the mood he is in. It depends also on whether you have a good or bad digestion, it depends on whether you are shut up in a room without proper ventilation or whether you are in the open air; it depends on whether you have a beautiful landscape before you; it depends on whether there is sunshine or rain! You are not aware of it, but you think all kinds of things, completely different according to a heap of things which have nothing to do with you!

And for this to become a coordinated, coherent, logical thought, a long thorough work is necessary.

Crystallising Your Thought

The usefulness of work is nothing else but [this]: to crystallise this mental power. For, what you learn (unless you put it in practice by some work or deeper studies), half of what you learn, at least, will vanish, disappear with time. But it will leave behind one thing: the capacity of crystallising your thought, making something clear out of it, something precise, exact and organised. And that is the true usefulness of work: to organise your cerebral capacity. . . .

I am going to explain it to you: when you have understood, it forms a little crystal in you, like a little shining point. And when you have put in many, many, many of these, then you will begin to be intelligent. That is the utility of work, not simply to stuff the head with a heap of things that take you nowhere.

*

Essentially, from the general point of view, particularly from the intellectual viewpoint, the most important thing is the capacity of attention and concentration, it is that which one must work at and develop. From the point of view of action (physical action), it is the will: you must work and build up an unshakable will. From the intellectual point of view, you must work and build up a power of concentration which nothing can shake. And if you have both, concentration and will, you will be a genius and nothing will resist you.

Remembering What You Learn

The true way so that [what you learn] remains is to understand, it is not to learn by heart. You learn something by heart, it is mechanical, you see; but after some time it will be effaced, unless you make use of it constantly. For example, you are made to learn by heart the multiplication tables; if you constantly use them, you will remember them, but if by chance for years you remain without using them, you will forget them completely. But if you understand the principle, you will be able to remember them. You see, the principle of multiplication, if you understand it with a mathematical sense, you will no longer need to learn it by heart, the operation will be done quite naturally in your brain; and for everything it is the same.

If you understand the thing, if you have the sense of the principle which is behind, you can remember it indefinitely, for hundreds of years if you live for hundreds of years; whereas something you have learnt by heart... after some time the brain cells multiply, are replaced, and some things are wiped out. . . . In one's life there are things which remain like landmarks, there are others which are totally effaced to the extent that one doesn't remember them at all, they are gone. But there are things like that, truly like milestones, like landmarks in life. Well, these things were conscious experiences, that is, they were understood; so the experience remains indefinitely, and with just a tiny movement of the consciousness you can bring it forward. But something that is learnt mechanically – unless, I tell you, you make use of it daily, it is effaced.

Knowledge Is within You

There is one thing certain about the mind and its workings; it is that you can understand only what you already know in your own inner self. What strikes you in a book is what you have already experienced deep within you. Men find a book or a teaching very wonderful and often you hear them say, "That is exactly what I myself feel and know, but I could not bring it out or express it as well as it is expressed here." When men come across a book of true knowledge, each finds himself there, and at every new reading he discovers things that he did not see in it at first; it opens to him each time a new field of knowledge that had till then escaped him in it. But that is because it reaches layers of knowledge that were waiting for expression in the subconscious in him; the expression has now been given by somebody else and much better than he could himself have done it. But, once expressed, he immediately recognises it and feels that it is the truth. The knowledge that seems to come to you from outside is only an occasion for bringing out the knowledge that is within you.

Reading which Awakens

For those who are seeking, who grope, who are not absolutely sure, who are pulled this way and that, have many interests in life, are not steady, stabilised in their will for realisation, it is very good to read, because it puts them in touch with the subject, it gives them some interest in the thing.

. . . There is a kind of reading which awakens in you an interest in the thing and can help you in the first seekings. Usually, even if one has had experiences one needs a contact of thought or idea with the thing so that the effort may be crystallised more consciously. But the more one knows, the more one must be absolutely sincere in his experience, that is, he must not use the formative power of his mind to imagine and so create the experience in himself. From the point of view of orientation it can be useful; but from the point of view of the experience, it takes away from it its dynamic value, it has not the intensity of an experience which comes because the moral and spiritual conditions necessary for it to occur have been fulfilled. There is the whole mental conditioning which is added and which takes away something of the spontaneity. All this is a matter of proportion. Each one must find the exact amount he needs, how much of reading, how much meditation, how much concentration, how much... It is different for each one.

Reading Sri Aurobindo's Writings

In a general and almost absolute way, if you truly wish to profit from these readings, as from all of Sri Aurobindo's writings, the best method is this: having gathered your consciousness and focussed your attention on what you are reading, you must establish a minimum of mental tranquillity – the best thing would be to obtain perfect silence – and achieve a state of immobility of the mind, immobility of the brain, I might say, so that the attention becomes as still and immobile as a mirror, like the surface of absolutely still water. Then what one has read passes through the surface and penetrates deep into the being where it is received with a minimum of distortion. Afterwards – sometimes long afterwards – it wells up again from the depths and manifests in the brain with its full power of comprehension, not as knowledge acquired from outside, but as a light one carried within.

In this way the faculty of understanding is at its highest, whereas if, while you read, the mind remains agitated and tries to understand at once what it is reading, you lose more than three-quarters of the force, the knowledge and the truth contained in the words. And if you are able to refrain from asking questions until this process of absorption and inner awakening is completed, well, then you will find that you have far fewer questions to ask because you will have a better understanding of what you have read.

Listening to Music

Mother, when one hears music, how should one truly hear it?

For this – if one can be completely silent, you see, silent and attentive, simply as though one were an instrument which has to record it – one does not move, and is only something that is listening – if one can be absolutely silent, absolutely still and like that, then the thing enters. And it is only later, some time later, that you can become aware of the effect, either of what it meant or the impression it had on you.

But the best way of listening is this. It is to be like a still mirror and very concentrated, very silent. In fact, we see people who truly love music... I have seen musicians listening to music, musicians, composers or players who truly love music, I have seen them listening to music... they sit completely still, you know, they are like that, they do not move at all. Everything, everything is like that. And if one can stop thinking, then it is very good, then one profits fully.... It is one of the methods of inner opening and one of the most powerful.

The Sense of Beauty

To do this yoga, one must have, at least a little, the sense of beauty. If one does not, one misses one of the most important aspects of the physical world.

There is this beauty, this dignity of soul – a thing about which I am very sensitive. It is a thing that moves me and evokes in me a great respect always.

Yes, this beauty of soul that is visible in the face, this kind of dignity, this harmony of integral realisation. When the soul becomes visible in the physical, it gives this dignity, this beauty, this majesty, the majesty that comes from one's being the Tabernacle. Then, even things that have no particular beauty put on a sense of eternal beauty, of *the* eternal beauty.

I have seen in this way faces that pass from one extreme to the other in a flash. Someone has this kind of beauty and harmony, this sense of divine dignity in the body; then suddenly there comes the perception of an obstacle, a difficulty, and the sense of fault, of indignity – and then, a sudden deformation in the appearance, a kind of decomposition of the features! And yet it is the same face. It was like a flash of lightning, and it was frightful. That kind of hideousness of torment and degradation – what has been translated in religions as "the torment of sin" – that gives you a face indeed! Even features that are beautiful in themselves become horrible. And it was the same features, the same person.

Then I saw how horrible the sense of sin is, how much it belongs to the world of falsehood.

A Sense of Gratitude

That kind of sense of gratitude that the Divine exists; that feeling of a marvelling thankfulness which truly fills you with a sublime joy at the fact that the Divine exists, that there is something in the universe which is the Divine, that it is not just the monstrosity we see, that there is the Divine, the Divine exists. And each time that the least thing puts you either directly or indirectly in contact with this sublime Reality of divine existence, the heart is filled with so intense, so marvellous a joy, with a gratitude that has a more delightful taste than anything else at all.

There is nothing which gives you a joy equal to that of gratitude. One hears a bird sing, sees a lovely flower, looks at a little child, observes an act of generosity, reads a beautiful sentence, looks at the setting sun, no matter what, suddenly this comes upon you, this kind of emotion – indeed so deep, so intense – that the world manifests the Divine, that there is something behind the world which is the Divine.

True Art

True art is intended to express the beautiful, but in close intimacy with the universal movement. The greatest nations and the most cultured races have always considered art as a part of life and made it subservient to life. Art was like that in Japan in its best moments; it was like that in all the best moments in the history of art. But most artists are like parasites growing on the margin of life; they do not seem to know that art should be the expression of the Divine in life and through life. In everything, everywhere, in all relations truth must be brought out in its all-embracing rhythm and every movement of life should be an expression of beauty and harmony. Skill is not art, talent is not art. Art is a living harmony and beauty that must be expressed in all the movements of existence. This manifestation of beauty and harmony is part of the Divine realisation upon earth, perhaps even its greatest part.

Art and Yoga

Does the work of an artist improve if he does Yoga?

The discipline of Art has at its centre the same principle as the discipline of Yoga. In both the aim is to become more and more conscious; in both you have to learn to see and feel something that is beyond the ordinary vision and feeling, to go within and bring out from there deeper things. Painters have to follow a discipline for the growth of the consciousness of their eyes, which in itself is almost a Yoga. If they are true artists and try to see beyond and use their art for the expression of the inner world, they grow in consciousness by this concentration, which is not other than the consciousness given by Yoga. Why then should not Yogic consciousness be a help to artistic creation? I have known some who had very little training and skill and yet through Yoga acquired a fine capacity in writing and painting.

A Living Art

When one paints a picture or composes music or writes poetry, each one has his own way of expression. Every painter, every musician, every poet, every sculptor has or ought to have a unique, personal contact with the Divine, and through the work which is his speciality, the art he has mastered, he must express this contact in his own way, with his own words, his own colours. For himself, instead of copying the outer form of Nature, he takes these forms as the covering of something else, precisely of his relationship with the realities which are behind, deeper, and he tries to make them express that. Instead of merely imitating what he sees, he tries to make them speak of what is behind them, and it is this which makes all the difference between a living art and just a flat copy of Nature.

Tell a Beautiful Story

Do not imaginary stories put you in contact with life, with truth?

Not always! And what does "contact with truth" mean? – there is a truth in a grain of sand. That means nothing.

Don't you think there are enough ugly things in the world without one's giving a picture of them in books? This is something which always used to surprise me, even when I was a child – life is so ugly, so full of mean, miserable, even at times repulsive things, what is the use of imagining yet worse things than are already there? If you imagined something more beautiful, a more beautiful life, that would be worth the trouble. People who take pleasure in writing ugly things show a great poverty of mind – it is always a sign of a poverty of mind. It is infinitely more difficult to tell a story beautiful from beginning to end than to write a story ending with a sensational event or a catastrophe. Many authors, if they had to write a story which ends happily, beautifully, would not be able to do it – they do not have enough imagination for that. Very few stories have an uplifting ending, almost all end in a failure – for a very simple reason, it is much more easy to fall than to rise. It is much more difficult to end one's story on a note of greatness and splendour, to make one's hero a genius seeking to transcend himself, because for that one must be a genius oneself, and this is not given to everybody.

MUNDANE AFFAIRS

The Materialism of Modern Times

At that time, the time of the Buddha, to live a spiritual life was a joy, a beatitude, the happiest state, which freed you from all the troubles of the world, all the sufferings, all the cares, making you happy, satisfied, contented.

It is the materialism of modern times that has turned spiritual effort into a hard struggle and a sacrifice, a painful renunciation of all the so-called joys of life.

This insistence on the exclusive reality of the physical world, of physical pleasures, physical joys, physical possessions, is the result of the whole materialistic tendency of human civilisation. It was unthinkable in ancient times. On the contrary, withdrawal, concentration, liberation from all material cares, consecration to the spiritual joy, that was happiness indeed.

From this point of view it is quite evident that humanity is far from having progressed; and those who were born into the world in the centres of materialistic civilisation have in their subconscient this horrible notion that only material realities are real and that to be concerned with things that are not material represents a wonderful spirit of sacrifice, an almost sublime effort. Not to be preoccupied from dawn to dusk and from dusk to dawn with all the little physical satisfactions, physical pleasures, physical sensations, physical preoccupations, is to bear evidence of a remarkable spirit.

Esau and Jacob

I don't know how many of you have read the Bible; it is not very entertaining to read it, and besides, it is very long, but still, in the Bible there is a story I have always liked very much. There were two brothers, if I am not mistaken, Esau and Jacob. Well, Esau was very hungry, that's the story, isn't it? I believe he was a hunter or something; anyway, the story goes like this. He came back home very hungry, and told Jacob he was very hungry, and he was so hungry that he said to him, "Listen, if you give me your mess of pottage" (Jacob had prepared some stew), "if you give me your mess of pottage I will give you my birthright." You know, one can understand the story quite superficially, but it has a very profound meaning: the birthright is the right of being the son of God. And so he was quite ready to give up his divine right because he was hungry, for a concrete, material thing, for food. This is a very old story, but it is eternally true.

Success and Failure

You must not judge things from an outer success or a semblance of defeat. We may say – and generally this is what almost always happens – we could say that the Divine gives what one desires, and of all lessons this is the best! For, if your desire is inconscient, obscure, egoistic, you increase the unconsciousness, the darkness and egoism within yourself; that is to say, this takes you farther and farther away from the truth, from consciousness and happiness. It takes you far away from the Divine. And for the Divine, naturally, only one thing is true – the divine Consciousness, the divine Union. And each time you put material things in front, you become more and more materialistic and go farther and farther away from full success.

But for the Truth, that other success is a terrible defeat.... You have exchanged truth for falsehood!

To judge from appearances and apparent success is precisely an act of complete ignorance. Even for the most hardened man, for whom everything has apparently been successful, even for him there is always a counterpart. And this kind of hardening of the being which is produced, this veil which is formed, a thicker and thicker veil, between the outer consciousness and the inner truth, becomes, one day or another, altogether intolerable. It is usually paid for very dearly – outer success.

(*Mother's voice becomes extremely deep.*) One must be *very* great, *very* pure, have a *very* high and *very* disinterested spiritual consciousness in order to be successful without being affected by it. *Nothing is more difficult than being successful. This, indeed, is the true test of life!*

When you do not succeed, quite naturally you turn back on yourself and within yourself, and you seek within yourself the consolation for your outer failure. And to those who have a flame within them – if the Divine really wants to help them, if they are mature enough to be helped, if they are ready to follow the path – blows will come one after another, because this helps! It is the most powerful, the most direct, most effective help. If you succeed, be on your guard, ask yourself: "At what price, what cost have I bought success? I hope it is not a step towards..."

There are those who have gone beyond this, those who are conscious of their soul, those who have given themselves entirely, those who – as I said – are absolutely pure, disinterested, and can succeed without its affecting and touching them; here, then, it is different. *But one must be very high to be able to bear success.* And after all, it is perhaps the last test which the Divine gives to anyone: "Now that you are noble, you are disinterested, you have no egoism, you belong only to me, I am going to make you triumph. We are going to see if you will hold out."

A Perfect Equality

When things happen which are not what we expect, what we hope for, what we want, which are contrary to our desires, in our ignorance we call them misfortunes and lament. But if we were to become a little wiser and observe the deeper consequences of these very same events, we would find that they are leading us rapidly towards the Divine, the Beloved; whereas easy and pleasant circumstances encourage us to dally on the path, to stop along the way to pluck the flowers of pleasure which present themselves to us and which we are too weak or not sincere enough to reject resolutely, so that our march forward is not delayed.

One must already be very strong, very far along the way, to be able to face success and the little enjoyments it brings without giving way. Those who can do this, those who are strong, do not run after success; they do not seek it, and accept it with indifference. For they know and appreciate the value of the lashes given by unhappiness and misfortune.

But ultimately the true attitude, the sign and proof that we are near the goal, is a perfect equality which enables us to accept success and failure, fortune and misfortune, happiness and sorrow with the same tranquil joy; for all these things become marvellous gifts that the Lord in his infinite solicitude showers upon us.

A Perfect Gift

What you are, give that; what you have, give that, and your gift will be perfect; from the spiritual point of view it will be perfect. This does not depend upon the amount of wealth you have or the number of capacities in your nature; it depends upon the perfection of your gift, that is to say, on the totality of your gift. I remember having read, in a book of Indian legends, a story like this. There was a very poor, very old woman who had nothing, who was quite destitute, who lived in a miserable little hut, and who had been given a fruit. It was a mango. She had eaten half of it and kept the other half for the next day, because it was something so marvellous that she did not often happen to get it – a mango. And then, when night fell, someone knocked at the rickety door and asked for hospitality. And this someone came in and told her he wanted shelter and was hungry. So she said to him, "Well, I have no fire to warm you, I have no blanket to cover you, and I have half a mango left, that is all I have, if you want it; I have eaten half of it." And it turned out that this someone was Shiva, and that she was filled with an inner glory, for she had made a perfect gift of herself and all she had.

I read that, I found it magnificent. Well, yes, this describes it vividly. It's exactly that.

The rich man, or even people who are quite well-off and have all sorts of things in life and give to the Divine what they have in surplus – for usually this is the gesture: one has a little more money than one needs, one has a few more things than one needs, and so, generously, one gives that to the Divine. It is better than giving nothing. But even if this "little more" than what they need represents lakhs of rupees, the gift is less perfect than the one of half the mango. For it is not by the quantity or the quality that it is measured: it is by the sincerity of the giving and the absoluteness of the giving.

Money Is Valuable When Spent

It is infinitely more difficult to be good, to be wise, to be intelligent and generous, to be more generous, you follow me, when one is rich than when one is poor. I have known many people in many countries, and the most generous people I have ever met in all the countries, were the poorest. And as soon as the pockets are full, one is caught by a kind of illness, which is a sordid attachment to money. I assure you it is a curse.

So the first thing to do when one has money is to give it. But as it is said that it should not be given without discernment, don't go and give it like those who practise philanthropy, because that fills them with a sense of their own goodness, their generosity and their own importance. You must act in a sattwic way, that is, make the best possible use of it. And so, each one must find in his highest consciousness what the best possible use of the money he has can be. And truly money has no value unless it circulates. For each and every one, money is valuable only when one has spent it. . . .

Wealth is a force – I have already told you this once – a force of Nature; and it should be a means of circulation, a power in movement, as flowing water is a power in movement. It is something which can serve to produce, to organise. It is a convenient means, because in fact it is only a means of making things circulate fully and freely.

This force should be in the hands of those who know how to make the best possible use of it, that is, as I said at the beginning, people who have abolished in themselves or in some way or other got rid of every personal desire and every attachment. To this should be added a vision vast enough to understand the needs of the earth, a knowledge complete enough to know how to organise all these needs and use this force by these means.

If, besides this, these beings have a higher spiritual knowledge, then they can utilise this force to construct gradually upon the earth what will be capable of manifesting the divine Power, Force and Grace.

Money Belongs to No One

The conflict about money is what might be called a "conflict of ownership", but the truth is that money belongs to no one. This idea of *possessing* money has warped everything. Money should not be a "possession": like power it is a means of action which is given to you, but you must use it according to... what we can call the "will of the Giver", that is, in an impersonal and enlightened way. If you are a good instrument for diffusing and utilising money, then it comes to you, and it comes to you in proportion to your capacity to use it as it is meant to be used. That is the true mechanism.

The true attitude is this: money is a force intended for the work on earth, the work required to prepare the earth to receive and manifest the divine forces, and it – that is, the power of utilising it – must come into the hands of those who have the clearest, most comprehensive and truest vision.

Production

It is said, "One cannot make a heap without making a hole", one cannot enrich oneself without impoverishing someone else. Is it true?

This is not quite correct. If one produces something, instead of an impoverishment it is an enrichment; simply one puts into circulation in the world something else having a value equivalent to that of money. But to say that one cannot make a heap without making a hole is all right for those who speculate, who do business on the Stock Exchange or in finance – there it is true. It is impossible to have a financial success in affairs of pure speculation without its being detrimental to another. But it is limited to this. Otherwise a producer does not make a hole if he heaps up money in exchange for what he produces. Surely there is a question of the value of the production, but if the production is truly an acquisition for the general human wealth, it does not make a hole, it increases this wealth. And in another way, not only in the material field, the same thing holds for art, for literature or science, for any production at all.

Have Respect for Things

How should we use things?

Ah, this is… First, to use things with an understanding of their true utility, the knowledge of their real use, with the utmost care so that they do not get spoilt and with the least confusion.

I am going to give you an example: you have a pair of scissors. There are scissors of all kinds, there are scissors for cutting paper, and there are scissors for cutting thread… Now if you have the pair of scissors which you need, use it for the thing it is made for. But I know people who, when they have a pair of scissors, use it without any discernment to cut anything at all, to cut small silk threads, and they try to cut a wire also with it or else they use it as a tool to open tins, you see; for anything whatever, where they need an instrument they get hold of their scissors and use them. So naturally, after quite a short while they come to me again and say, "Oh, my pair of scissors is spoilt, I would like to have another." And they are very much surprised when I tell them, "No, you won't have another, because you have spoilt this one, because you have used it badly." This is just one example, I could give many others.

People use something which gets dirty and is spoilt in becoming dirty, or they forget to clean it or neglect it, because all this takes time.

There is a kind of respect for the object one has, which must make one treat it with much consideration and try to preserve it as long as possible, not because one is attached to it and desires it, but because an object is something respectable which has sometimes cost a lot of effort and labour in the producing and so must as a result be considered with the respect due to the work and effort put into it. . . .

Many a time I say, "No, use what you have. Try to make the best possible use of it. Don't throw away things uselessly, don't ask uselessly. Try to do with what you have, putting into it all the care, all the order, all the necessary method, and avoiding confusion."

The Problem of Food

If one wishes to pass from this ordinary life to a higher one, the problem [of food] begins to become interesting; and if, after having come to a higher life, one tries to prepare oneself for the transformation, then it becomes very important. For there certainly are foods which help the body to become subtle and others which keep it in a state of animality. But it is only at that particular time that this becomes very important, not before; and before reaching that moment, there are many other things to do. Certainly it is better to purify one's mind and purify one's vital before thinking of purifying one's body. For even if you take all possible precautions and live physically taking care not to absorb anything except what will help to subtilise your body, if your mind and vital remain in a state of desire, inconscience, darkness, passion and all the rest, that won't be of any use at all. Only, your body will become weak, dislocated from the inner life and one fine day it will fall ill.

One must begin from inside, I have already told you this once. One must begin from above, first purify the higher and then purify the lower. I am not saying that one must indulge in all sorts of degrading things in the body. That's not what I am telling you. Don't take it as an advice not to exercise control over your desires! It isn't that at all. But what I mean is, do not try to be an angel in the body if you are not already just a little of an angel in your mind and vital; for that would dislocate you in a different way from the usual one, but not one that is better. We said the other day that what is most important is to keep the equilibrium. Well, to keep the equilibrium everything must progress at the same time. You must not leave one part of your being in darkness and try to bring the other into light. You must take great care not to leave any corner dark.

Eat Reasonably

The best thing is not to think about [food] but to regulate one's life automatically enough not to need to think of eating. You eat at fixed hours, eat reasonably, you don't even need to think of the food when you are taking it; you must eat calmly, that's all, quietly, with concentration, and when you do not eat you must never think about it. You must not eat too much, because then you will have to think about your digestion, and it will be very unpleasant for you and will make you waste much time. You must eat just... you must put an end to all desire, all attraction, all movements of the vital, because when you eat simply because the body needs to eat, the body will tell you absolutely precisely and exactly when it has had enough; you see, when one is not moved by a vital desire or mental ideas, one grasps this with surety. "Now it is enough," says the body, "I don't want any more." So one stops.

Offer Your Food to the Divine

As long as our body is compelled to take in foreign matter in order to subsist, it will absorb at the same time a considerable amount of inert and unconscious forces or those having a rather undesirable consciousness, and this alchemy must take place inside the body. We were speaking of the kinds of consciousness absorbed with food, but there is also the inconscience that's absorbed with food – quite a deal of it. And that is why in many yogas there was the advice to offer to the Divine what one was going to eat before eating it (*Mother makes a gesture of offering, hands joined, palms open*). It consists in calling the Divine down into the food before eating it. One offers it to Him – that is, one puts it in contact with the Divine, so that it may be under the divine influence when one eats it. It is very useful, it is very good. If one knows how to do it, it is very useful, it considerably reduces the work of inner transformation which has to be done.

Smoking, Drinking and Drugs

Some people believe that smoking, drinking, etc. will form part of the life of tomorrow. That is their business. If they want to go through this experience, let them do it. They will realise that they are imprisoning themselves in their own desires. But anyway, I am not a moralist, not at all, at all, at all. It is their own business. It is their own business. If they want to go through this experience, let them do it. But the Ashram is not the place for it. Thank God, at the Ashram we have learnt that life is something else. True life is not the satisfaction of desires. I can affirm from experience that all the experiences brought by drugs, all that contact with the invisible world, can be had in a much better, more conscious and controlled way without drugs. Only, one must control oneself. It is more difficult than swallowing poison. But I am not going to preach.

Drinking and Drugs: Self-control

There are human beings also who indulge in vice – one vice or another, like drinking or drug-injections – and who know very well that this is leading them to destruction and death. But they choose to do it, knowingly.

They have no control over themselves.

There is always a moment when everyone has self-control. And if one had not said "Yes" once, if one had not taken the decision, one would not have done it.

There is not one human being who has not the energy and capacity to resist something imposed upon him – if he is left free to do so. People tell you, "I can't do otherwise" – it is because in the depths of their heart they *do not want* to do otherwise; they have accepted to be the slaves of their vice. There is a moment when one accepts.

Tobacco and Alcohol

Why do tobacco and alcohol destroy the memory and will?

Why? Because they do so. There is no moral reason. It is a fact. There is a poison in alcohol, there is a poison in tobacco; and this poison goes into the cells and damages them. Alcohol is never expelled, so to say; it accumulates in a certain part of the brain, and then, after the accumulation, these cells no longer function at all – some people even go mad because of it, that is what is called *delirium tremens*, the result of having swallowed too much alcohol which is not absorbed but remains in this way concentrated in the brain. And it is so radical even that... There is a province in

France, for instance, which produces wine, a wine with a very low percentage of alcohol: I believe it is four or five per cent, a very low percentage, you understand; and these people, because they make it, drink wine as one drinks water. They drink it neat, and after some time they become ill. They have cerebral disorders. I knew people of this kind, the brain was disordered, didn't function any more. And tobacco – nicotine is a very serious poison. It is a poison that destroys the cells. I have said that it is a slow poison because one doesn't feel it immediately except when one smokes for the first time and it makes one very ill. And this should make you understand that it ought not to be done. Only, people are so stupid that they think it is a weakness and so continue until they get used to the poison. And the body no longer reacts, it allows itself to be destroyed without reacting: you get rid of the reaction.

It is the same thing physically as morally. When you do something you ought not to do and your psychic tells you in its still small voice not to do it, then if you do it in spite of that, after a while it will no longer tell you anything, and you will no longer have any inner reactions at all to your bad actions, because you have refused to listen to the voice when it spoke to you. And then, naturally, you go from bad to worse and tumble into the hole. Well, for tobacco it is the same thing: the first time the body reacts violently, it vomits, it tells you, "I don't want it at any cost." You compel it with your mental and vital stupidity, you force it to do so; it doesn't react any longer and so lets itself be poisoned gradually until it decomposes. The functioning deteriorates; it is the nerves that are affected; they no longer transmit the will because they are affected, they are poisoned. They no longer have the strength to transmit the will. And finally people begin to tremble, they have nervous movements. There are quite a few, one doesn't need to go very far to find them. And they are like that only because they have committed excesses: they drank and smoked. And when they lift an object, their hands shake (*gesture*). That's what one gets by doing this.

Sex and Yoga

There is another danger; it is in connection with the sex impulses. Yoga in its process of purification will lay bare and throw up all hidden impulses and desires in you. And you must learn not to hide things nor leave them aside, you have to face them and conquer and remould them. The first effect of Yoga, however, is to take away the mental control, and the hungers that lie dormant are suddenly set free, they rush up and invade the being. So long as this mental control has not been replaced by the Divine control, there is a period of transition when your sincerity and surrender will be put to the test. The strength of such impulses as those of sex lies usually in the fact that people take too much notice of them; they protest too vehemently and endeavour to control them by coercion, hold them within and sit upon them. But the more you think of a thing and say, "I don't want it, I don't want it", the more you are bound to it. What you should do is to keep the thing away from you, to dissociate from it, take as little notice of it as possible and, even if you happen to think of it, remain indifferent and unconcerned.

The impulses and desires that come up by the pressure of Yoga should be faced in a spirit of detachment and serenity, as something foreign to yourself or belonging to the outside world. They should be offered to the Divine, so that the Divine may take them up and transmute them.

If you have once opened yourself to the Divine, if the power of the Divine has once come down into you and yet you try to keep to the old forces, you prepare troubles and difficulties and dangers for yourself. You must be vigilant and see that you do not use the Divine as a cloak for the satisfaction of your desires.

The Sexual Impulse

Humanity has the sexual impulse in a way altogether natural, spontaneous and, I would say, legitimate. This impulse will naturally and spontaneously disappear with animality. Many other things will disappear, as for example the need to eat and perhaps also the need to sleep in the way we sleep now. But the most conscious impulse in a superior humanity, which has continued as a source of... bliss is a big word, but joy, delight – is certainly the sexual activity, and that will have absolutely no reason for existence in the functions of Nature when the need to create in that way will no longer exist. Therefore, the capacity of entering into relation with the joy of life will rise by one step or will be oriented differently. But what the ancient spiritual aspirants had sought on principle – sexual negation – is an absurd thing, because this must be only for those who have gone beyond this stage and no longer have animality in them. And it must drop off naturally, without effort and without struggle. To make of it a centre of conflict and struggle is ridiculous. It is only when the consciousness ceases to be human that it drops off quite naturally. Here also there is a transition which may be somewhat difficult, because the beings of transition are always in an unstable equilibrium; but within oneself there is a kind of flame and a need which makes it not painful – it is not a painful effort, it is something that one can do with a smile. But to seek to impose it upon those who are not ready for this transition is absurd.

It is common sense. They are human, but they must not pretend that they are not.

It is only when spontaneously the impulse becomes impossible for you, when you feel that it is something painful and contrary to your deeper need that it becomes easy; then, well, externally you cut these bonds and it is finished.

Know How to Love

It is said that to become conscious of divine Love all other love has to be abandoned. What is the best way of rejecting the other love which clings so obstinately (laughter) *and does not easily leave us?*

To go through it. Ah!

To go through, to see what is behind it, not to stop at the appearance, not to be satisfied with the outer form, to look for the principle which is behind this love, and not be content until one has found the *origin* of the feeling in oneself. Then the outer form will crumble of itself and you will be in contact with the divine Love which is behind all things.

That is the best way.

To want to get rid of the one in order to find the other is very difficult. It is almost impossible. For human nature is so limited, so full of contradictions and so exclusive in its movements that if one wants to reject love in its lower form, that is to say, human love as human beings experience it, if one makes an inner effort to reject it, one usually rejects the entire capacity of feeling love and becomes like a stone. And then sometimes one has to wait for years or centuries before there is a reawakening in oneself of the capacity to receive and manifest love.

Therefore, the best way when love comes, in whatever form it may be, is to try and pierce through its outer appearance and find the divine principle which is behind and which gives it existence. Naturally, it is full of snares and difficulties, but it is more effective. That is to say, instead of ceasing to love because one loves wrongly, one must cease to love wrongly and want to love well.

For instance, love between human beings, in all its forms, the love of parents for children, of children for parents, of brothers and sisters, of friends and lovers, is all tainted with ignorance, selfishness and all the other defects which are man's ordinary drawbacks; so instead of completely ceasing to love – which, besides, is very difficult as Sri Aurobindo says, which would simply dry up the heart and serve no end – one must learn how to love better: to love with devotion, with self-giving, self-abnegation, and to struggle, not against love itself, but against its distorted forms: against all forms of monopolising, of attachment, possessiveness, jealousy, and all the feelings which accompany these main movements. Not to want to possess, to dominate; and not to want to impose one's will, one's whims, one's desires; not to want to take, to receive, but to give; not to insist on the other's response, but be content with one's own love; not to seek one's personal interest and joy and the fulfilment of one's personal desire, but to be satisfied with the giving of one's love and affection; and not to ask for any response. Simply to be happy to love, nothing more.

If you do that, you have taken a great stride forward and can, through this attitude, gradually advance farther in the feeling itself, and realise one day that love is not something personal, that love is a universal divine feeling which manifests through you more or less finely, but which in its essence is something divine.

The first step is to stop being selfish. For everyone it is the same thing, not only for those who want to do yoga but also in ordinary life: if one wants to know how to love, one must not love oneself first and above all selfishly; one must give oneself to the object of love without exacting anything in return. This discipline is elementary in order to surmount oneself and lead a life which is not altogether gross.

As for yoga we may add something else: it is as I said in the beginning, the will to pierce through this limited and human form of love and discover the principle of divine Love which is behind it. Then one is sure to get a result. This is better than drying up one's heart. It is perhaps a little more difficult but it is better in every way, for like this, instead of egoistically making others suffer, well, one may leave them quiet in their own movement and only make an effort to transform oneself without imposing one's will on others, which even in ordinary life is a step towards something higher and a little more harmonious.

To Know What Love Is

If one wants to know what love is, one must love the Divine. Then there is a chance of knowing what love is. I have said that one grows into the likeness of what one loves. So if one loves the

Divine, gradually, through this effort of love, one grows more and more like the Divine, and then one can be identified with the divine love and know what it is, otherwise one can't.

Inevitably, love between two human beings, whatever it may be, is always made of ignorance, lack of understanding, weakness and that terrible sense of separation. It is as though one wanted to enter the presence of a unique Splendour and that the first thing one did was to put a curtain, two curtains, three curtains between oneself and that Splendour, and one is quite surprised to have only a vague impression and not at all the thing itself. The first thing to do is to remove the curtains, to take them all away, to go through and find oneself in the presence of the Splendour. And then you will know what that Splendour is. But if you put veil after veil between it and yourself, you will never see it. You may have a sort of vague feeling like "Oh! there is something", but that is all.

Divine Love Is There

Divine Love is there always in all its intensity, a formidable power. But most people – ninety-nine per cent – do not feel anything at all! What they feel of it is exclusively in proportion to what they are, to their capacity of receiving. Imagine, for instance, that you are bathing in an atmosphere all vibrant with divine Love – you are not at all aware of it. Sometimes, very rarely, for a few seconds there is suddenly the feeling of "something". Then you say, "Oh, divine Love came to me!" What a joke! It is just that you were simply, for some reason or other, a wee bit open, so you felt it. But it is there, always, like the divine Consciousness. It is the same thing, it is there, all the time, in its full intensity; but one is not even aware of it; or else in this way, spasmodically: suddenly one is in a good state, so one feels something and says, "Oh, the divine Consciousness, divine Love have turned to me, have come to me!" It is not at all like that. One has just a tiny little opening, very tiny, at times like a pin-head, and naturally that force rushes in. For it is like an active atmosphere; as soon as there is a possibility of being

received, it is received. But this is so for all divine things. They are
there, only one does not receive them, for one is closed up,
blocked, one is busy with other things most of the time. Most of
the time one is full of oneself. So, as one is full of oneself, there is
no place for anything else. One is very actively (*laughing*) busy
with other things. One is filled with things, there is no place for the
Divine.

But He is there.

Before Going to Sleep

One thing you can do in all security is, before going to sleep, to
concentrate, relax all tension in the physical being, try... that is, in
the body try so that the body lies like a soft rag on the bed, that it is
no longer something with twitchings and cramps; to relax it
completely as though it were a kind of thing like a rag. And then,
the vital: to calm it, calm it as much as you can, make it as quiet, as
peaceful as possible. And then the mind also – the mind, try to
keep it like that, without any activity. You must put upon the brain
the force of great peace, great quietude, of silence if possible, and
not follow ideas actively, not make any effort, nothing, nothing;
you must relax all movement there too, but relax it in a kind of
silence and quietude as great as possible.

Once you have done all this, you may add either a prayer or an
aspiration in accordance with your nature to ask for the consciousness and peace and to be protected against all the adverse
forces throughout the sleep, to be in a concentration of quiet
aspiration and in the protection; ask the Grace to watch over your
sleep; and then go to sleep. This is to sleep in the best possible
conditions. What happens afterwards depends on your inner
impulses, but if you do this persistently, night after night, night
after night, after some time it will have its effect.

Stopping Illness

Sweet Mother, when one sees an illness coming, how can one stop it?

Ah! First of all, you must not want it, and nothing in the body must want it. You must have a very strong will not to be ill. This is the first condition.

The second condition is to call the light, a light of equilibrium, a light of peace, quietude and balance, and to push it into all the cells of the body, enjoining them not to be afraid, because that again is another condition.

First, not to want to be ill, and then not to be afraid of illness. You must neither attract it nor tremble. You must not want illness at all. But you must not because of fear not want it; you must not be afraid; you must have a calm certitude and a complete trust in the power of the Grace to shelter you from everything, and then think of something else, not be concerned about this any longer. When you have done these two things, refusing the illness with all your will and infusing a confidence which completely eliminates the fear in the cells of the body, and then busying yourself with something else, not thinking any longer about the illness, forgetting that it exists... there, if you know how to do that, you may even be in contact with people who have contagious diseases, and yet you do not catch them. But you must know how to do this.

Many people say, "Oh, yes, here I am not afraid." They don't have any fear in the mind, their mind is not afraid, it is strong, it is not afraid; but the body trembles, and one doesn't know it, because it is in the cells of the body that the trembling goes on. It trembles with a terrible anxiety and this is what attracts the illness. It is there that you must put the force and the quietude of a perfect peace and an absolute trust in the Grace.

The Dying Man

Once one has left his body, whether he is conscious or unconscious, whether he is developed or not, one always goes out into
the same domain to begin with – unless one is a yogi who can do
what he likes with himself, but that, you know, is so rare a case that
one can't consider it. All men when they leave their body are flung
into a domain of the lower vital which has nothing particularly
pleasant about it. . . .

The most important thing in this case is the last state of
consciousness in which one was while both were joined together,
when the vital being and the body were still united. So the last state
of consciousness, one may say the last desire or the last hope or the
last aspiration, has a colossal importance for the first impact the
being has with the invisible world. And here the responsibility of
the people around the dying man is much greater than they think.
If they can help him to enter his highest consciousness, they will do
him the greatest service they can. But usually what they do is to
cling to him as much as they can, and to pull him towards them
with a fierce selfishness; the result, you see, is that instead of being
able to withdraw in a slightly higher consciousness which will
protect him in his exit, he is gripped by material things and it is a
terrible inner battle to free himself from both his body and his
attachments.

Religious Ceremony

In the invisible world hardly any beings love to be worshipped,
except those of the vital. These, as I said, are quite pleased by it.
And then, it gives them importance. They are puffed up with pride
and feel very happy, and when they can get a herd of people to
worship them they are quite satisfied.

But if you take real divine beings, this is not at all something
they value. They do not like to be worshipped. No, it does not give
them any special pleasure at all! Don't think they are happy, for

they have no pride. It is because of pride that a man likes to be worshipped; if a man has no pride he doesn't like to be worshipped; and if, for instance they see a good intention or a fine feeling or a movement of unselfishness or enthusiasm, a joy, a spiritual joy, these things have for them an infinitely greater value than prayers and acts of worship and pujas...

I assure you what I am telling you is very serious: if you seat a real god in a chair and oblige him to remain there all the while you are doing puja, he may perhaps have a little fun watching you do it, but it certainly gives him no satisfaction. None at all! He does not feel either flattered or happy or glorified by your puja. You must get rid of that idea. . . .

Religious ceremony! For example, there are so many of these entities called Kali – who are given, besides, quite terrible appearances – so many are even placed in houses as the family-goddess; they are full of a terrible vital force! I knew people who were so frightened of the Kali they had at home that indeed they trembled to make the least mistake, for when catastrophes came they thought it was Kali who sent them! It is a frightful thing, thought. I know them, those entities. I know them very well, but they are vital beings, vital forms which, so to say, are given a form by human thought, and what forms! And to think that men worship such terrible and monstrous things; and what's more that these poor gods are given, are paid the compliment of believing that it is...

From this point of view, it is good that for some time men get out of this religious atmosphere, so full of fear, and this sort of blind, superstitious submission of which the hostile forces have taken a dreadful advantage. The period of denial, positivism, is from this viewpoint quite indispensable in order to free men from superstition. It is only when one comes out of that and the abject submission to monstrous vital forces that one can rise to truly spiritual heights and there become the collaborator and true instrument of the forces of Truth, the real Consciousness, the true Power.

One must leave all this far behind before one can climb higher.

Religious Exercises

Sweet Mother, are religious exercises very important for those who have an ordinary consciousness?

Religious exercises? I don't know! What do you mean by religious exercises?

Japa, etc.

Oh, those things! If it helps you, it is all right. If it doesn't help you, it is just... This is one of those altogether relative things. It is altogether relative. Its value lies only in the effect it has on you and the extent to which you believe in it. If it helps you to concentrate, it is good. The ordinary consciousness always does it just through superstition, with the idea that "If I do this, if I go to the temple or church once a week, if I offer prayers, something very fine will happen to me." This is superstition, spread all over the world, but it has no value at all from the spiritual point of view.

Spiritual Life: East and West

Whatever difference there is between the West and the East in relation to spiritual life lies not in the inner being or nature, which is an invariable and constant thing, but in the mental habits, in the modes of outer expression and presentation which are the result of education and environment and other external conditions. All people, whether occidental or oriental, are alike in their deepest feelings; they are different in their way of thinking. Sincerity, for example, is a quality which is the same everywhere. Those who are sincere, to whichever nation they belong, are all sincere in the same way. Only the forms given to this sincerity vary. The mind works in different ways in different peoples, but the heart is the same everywhere; the heart is a much truer reality, and the differences belong to the superficial parts. As soon as you go deep enough, you meet something that is one in all. All meet in the Divine.

WORDS, OPINIONS, JUDGMENTS

Your Mantra

When you are playing and suddenly become aware that something is going wrong – you are making mistakes, are inattentive, sometimes opposing currents come across what you are doing – if you develop the habit, automatically at this moment, of calling as by a mantra, of repeating a word, that has an extraordinary effect. You choose your mantra; or rather, one day it comes to you spontaneously in a moment of difficulty. At a time when things are very difficult, when you have a sort of anguish, anxiety, when you don't know what is going to happen, suddenly this springs up in you, the word springs up in you. For each one it may be different. But if you mark this and each time you face a difficulty you repeat it, it becomes irresistible. For instance, if you feel you are about to fall ill, if you feel you are doing badly what you are doing, if you feel something evil is going to attack you, then.... But it must be a spontaneity in the being, it must spring up from you without your needing to think about it: you choose your mantra because it is a spontaneous expression of your aspiration; it may be one word, two or three words, a sentence, that depends on each one, but it must be a sound which awakens in you a certain condition. Then, when you have that, I assure you that you can pass through everything without difficulty. . . . The best is when the word comes to you spontaneously: you call in a moment of great difficulty (mental, vital, physical, emotional, whatever it may be) and suddenly that springs up in you, two or three words, like magical words. You must remember these and form the habit of repeating them in moments when difficulties come. If you form the habit, one day it will come to you spontaneously: when the difficulty comes, at the same time the mantra will come. Then you will see that the results are wonderful. But it must not be an artificial thing or something you arbitrarily decide: "I shall use those words"; nor should somebody else tell you, "Oh! you know,

this is very good" – it is perhaps very good for him but not for
everyone.

Say Only the Indispensable Words

I suggest that every one of you should try – oh! not for long, just
for one hour a day – to say nothing but the absolutely indispensable words. Not one more, not one less.

Take one hour of your life, the one which is most convenient for
you, and during that time observe yourself closely and say only the
absolutely indispensable words.

At the outset, the first difficulty will be to know what is
absolutely indispensable and what is not. It is already a study in
itself and every day you will do better.

Next, you will see that so long as one says nothing, it is not
difficult to remain absolutely silent, but as soon as you begin to
speak, always or almost always you say two or three or ten or
twenty useless words which it was not at all necessary to say.

Gossiping Degrades You

There is a state in which a simple conversation which obliges you
to remain on the level of ordinary life gives you a headache, turns
your stomach and, if it continues, may give you a fever. I am
speaking of course about the gossip-type of conversations. I
believe that apart from a few exceptions, everybody indulges in
this exercise and talks of things about which he should keep silent
or chatters about other things. It becomes so natural that you are
not troubled by it. But if you continue in this way, you hinder your
consciousness completely from rising up; you bind yourself with
iron chains to the ordinary consciousness and the work in the
subconscious is not done or has not even begun. Those who want
to rise up have already enough difficulties without looking for
encouragements outside.

Naturally, the effort to keep the consciousness at a high level is tiring in the beginning, like the exercices you do to develop your muscles. But you do not give up gymnastics because of that! So mentally also you must do the same thing. You must not allow your mind to stoop low: gossiping degrades you and, if you want to do yoga, you must abstain from it, that's all.

Widening Your Thought

You are with someone. This person tells you something, you tell him the contrary (as it usually happens, simply through a spirit of contradiction) and you begin arguing. Naturally, you will never come to any point, except a quarrel if you are ill-natured. But instead of doing that, instead of remaining in your own ideas or your own words, if you tell yourself: "Wait a little, I am going to try and see why he said that to me. Yes, why did he tell me that?" And you concentrate: "Why, why, why?" You stand there, just like that, trying. The other person continues speaking, doesn't he? – and is very happy too, for you don't contradict him any longer! He talks profusely and is sure he has convinced you. Then you concentrate more and more on what he is saying, and with the feeling that gradually, through his words, you are entering his mind. When you enter his head, suddenly you enter into his way of thinking, and next, just imagine, you understand why he is speaking to you thus! And then, if you have a fairly swift intelligence and put what you have just come to understand alongside what you had known before, you have the two ways together, and so can find the truth reconciling both. And here you have truly made progress. And this is the best way of widening one's thought.

If you are beginning an argument, keep quiet immediately, instantaneously. You must be silent, say nothing at all, and then try to see the thing as the other person sees it – that won't make you forget your own way of seeing it, not at all! but you will be able to put both of them together. And you will truly have made progress, a real progress.

Meddling With Others' Affairs

What is the best attitude? Is it an attitude of intervention or an attitude of non-interference? Which is better?

Ah, that's just it, to intervene you must be sure that you are right; you must be sure that your vision of things is superior, preferable or truer than the vision of the other person or people. Then it is always wiser not to intervene – people intervene without rhyme or reason, simply because they are in the habit of giving their opinion to others.

Even when you have the vision of the true thing, it is *very rarely* wise to intervene. It only becomes indispensable when someone wants to do something which will necessarily lead to a catastrophe. Even then, intervention (*smiling*) is not always very effective.

In fact, intervention is justified only when you are absolutely sure that you have the vision of truth. Not only that, but also a clear vision of the consequences. To intervene in someone else's actions, one must be a prophet – a prophet. And a prophet with total goodness and compassion. One must even have the vision of the consequences that the intervention will have in the destiny of the other person. People are always giving each other advice: "Do this, don't do that." I see it: they have no idea how much confusion they create, how they increase confusion and disorder. And sometimes they impair the normal development of the individual.

I consider that opinions are always dangerous and most often absolutely worthless.

You should not meddle with other people's affairs, unless first of all you are infinitely wiser than they are – of course, one always thinks that one is wiser! – but I mean in an objective way and not according to your own opinion; unless you see further and better and are yourself above all passions, desires and blind reactions. You must be above all these things yourself to have the right to intervene in someone else's life – even when he asks you to do so. And when he does not, it is simply meddling with something which is not your business.

Judging Others

Unless your vision is *constantly* the vision of the Divine in all things, you have not only no right but no capacity to judge the state which others are in. And to pronounce a judgment on someone without having this vision spontaneously, effortlessly, is precisely an example of the mental presumptuousness of which Sri Aurobindo always spoke.... And it so happens that one who has the vision, the consciousness, who is capable of seeing the truth in all things, never feels the need to judge anything whatever. For he understands everything and knows everything. Therefore, once and for all, you must tell yourselves that the moment you begin to judge things, people, circumstances, you are in the most total human ignorance.

In short, one could put it like this: when one understands, one no longer judges and when one judges, it means that one doesn't know.

Humanity Is Unable to Judge

The conclusion is always the same: the only true attitude is one of humility, of silent respect before what one does not know, and of inner aspiration to come out of one's ignorance. One of the things which would make humanity progress most would be for it to respect what it does not know, to acknowledge willingly that it does not know and is therefore unable to judge. We constantly do just the opposite. We pass final judgments on things of which we have no knowledge whatsoever, and say in a peremptory manner, "This is possible. That is impossible", when we do not even know what it is we are speaking of. And we put on superior airs because we doubt things of which we have never had any knowledge.

Men believe that doubt is a sign of superiority, whereas it is really a sign of inferiority.

Scepticism and doubt are two of the greatest obstacles to progress; they add presumptuousness to ignorance.

VIRTUE, PURITY, FREEDOM

Laugh with the Lord

Virtue has always spent its time eliminating whatever it found bad in life, and if all the virtues of the various countries of the world had been put together, very few things would remain in existence.

Virtue claims to seek perfection, but perfection is a totality. So the two movements contradict each other. A virtue that eliminates, reduces, fixes limits, and a perfection that accepts everything, rejects nothing but puts each thing in its place, obviously cannot agree.

Taking life seriously generally consists of two movements: the first one is to give importance to things that probably have none, and the second is to want life to be reduced to a certain number of qualities that are considered pure and worthy of existence. In some people. . . this virtue becomes dry, arid, grey, aggressive and it finds fault everywhere, in everything that is joyful and free and happy.

The only way to make life perfect – I mean here, life on earth, of course – is to look at it from high enough to see it as a whole, not only in its present totality, but in the whole of the past, present and future: what it has been, what it is and what it will be – one must be able to see everything at once. Because that is the only way to put everything in its place. Nothing can be eliminated, nothing *should* be eliminated, but each thing must be in its place in total harmony with all the rest. And then all these things that seem so "bad", so "reprehensible", so "unacceptable" to the puritan mind, would become movements of delight and freedom in a totally divine life. And then nothing would prevent us from knowing, understanding, feeling and living this wonderful laughter of the Supreme who takes infinite delight in watching Himself live infinitely.

This delight, this wonderful laughter that dissolves every shadow, every pain, every suffering! You only have to go deep enough within yourself to find the inner Sun, to let yourself be flooded by it; and then there is nothing but a cascade of harmonious, luminous, sunlit laughter, which leaves no room for any shadow or pain. . . .

And this Sun, this Sun of divine laughter is at the centre of all things, the truth of all things: we must learn to see it, to feel it, to live it.

And for that, let us avoid people who take life seriously; they are very boring people.

As soon as the atmosphere becomes grave you can be sure that something is wrong, that there is a troubling influence, an old habit trying to reassert itself, which should not be accepted. All this regret, all this remorse, the feeling of being unworthy, of being at fault – and then one step further and you have the sense of sin. Oh! to me it all seems to belong to another age, an age of darkness.

But everything that persists, that tries to cling and endure, all these prohibitions and this habit of cutting life in two – into small things and big things, the sacred and the profane.... "What!" say the people who profess to follow a spiritual life, "how can you make such little things, such insignificant things the object of spiritual experience?" And yet this is an experience that becomes more and more concrete and real, even materially; it's not that there are "some things" where the Lord is and "some things" where He is not. The Lord is *always* there. He takes nothing seriously, everything amuses Him and He plays with you, if you know how to play. You do not know how to play, people do not know how to play. But how well He knows how to play! How well He plays! With everything, with the smallest things: you have some things to put on the table? Don't feel that you have to think and arrange, no, let's play: let's put this one here and that one there, and this one like that. And then another time it's different again.... What a good game and such fun!

So, it is agreed, we shall try to learn how to laugh with the Lord.

The Need to Be Virtuous

Basically, this kind of will for purity, for good, in men – which expresses itself in the ordinary mentality as the need to be virtuous – is the *great obstacle* to true self-giving. This is the origin of Falsehood and even more the very source of hypocrisy – the refusal to accept to take upon oneself one's own share of the burden of difficulties. . . .

Do not try to appear virtuous. See how much you are united, one with everything that is anti-divine. Take your share of the burden, accept, yourselves, to be impure and false and in that way you will be able to take up the Shadow and offer it. And in so far as you are capable of taking it and offering it, then things will change.

Do not try to be among the pure. Accept to be with those who are in darkness and give it all with total love.

Total Purity

Sweet Mother, to be pure means what?

To be pure, what does it mean? One is truly perfectly pure only when the whole being, in all its elements and all its movements, adheres fully, exclusively, to the divine Will. This indeed is total purity. It does not depend on any moral or social law, any mental convention of any kind. It depends exclusively on this: when all the elements and all the movements of the being adhere exclusively and totally to the divine Will.

. . . As soon as you speak of purity, a moral monument comes in front of you which completely falsifies your notion. And note that it is infinitely easier to be moral from the social point of view than to be moral from the spiritual point of view. To be moral from the social viewpoint one has only to pay good attention to do nothing which is not approved of by others; this may be somewhat difficult, but still it is not impossible; and one may be, as I said, a monument of insincerity and impurity while doing this; whereas to be pure from the spiritual point of view means a vigilance, a consciousness, a sincerity that stand all tests.

Now, I may put you on your guard against... people who live in their vital consciousness and say, "I indeed am above moral laws, I follow a higher law, I am free from all moral laws." And they say this because they want to indulge in all irregularities. These people, then, have a double impurity: they have spiritual impurity and in addition social impurity. And these usually have a very good opinion of themselves, and they assert their wish to live their life with an unequalled impudence. But such people we don't want.

Yet usually the people whom I have found most difficult to convert are very respectable people. I am sorry, but I have had much more difficulty with respectable people than with those who were not so, for they had such a good opinion of themselves that it was impossible to open them. But the true thing *is* difficult. That is to say, one must be very vigilant and very self-controlled, very patient, and have a never-failing goodwill. One must not neglect having a small dose of humility, a sufficient one, and one must never be satisfied with the sincerity one has. One must always want more.

The Right to Be Free

Many times in his writings, particularly in *The Synthesis of Yoga*, Sri Aurobindo warns us against the imaginings of those who believe they can do sadhana without rigorous self-control and who heed all sorts of inspirations, which lead them to a dangerous imbalance where all their repressed, hidden, secret desires come out into the open under the pretence of liberation from ordinary conventions and ordinary reason.

One can be free only by soaring to the heights, high above human passions. Only when one has achieved a higher, selfless freedom and done away with all desires and impulses does one have the right to be free.

But neither should people who are very reasonable, very moral according to ordinary social laws, think themselves wise, for their wisdom is an illusion and holds no profound truth.

One who would break the law must be above the law. One who would ignore conventions must be above conventions. One who would despise all rules must be above all rules. And the motive of this liberation should never be a personal, egoistic one: the desire to satisfy an ambition, aggrandise one's personality, through a feeling of superiority, out of contempt for others, to set oneself above the herd and regard it with condescension. Be on your guard when you feel yourself superior and look down on others ironically, as if to say, "I'm no longer made of such stuff." That's when you go off the track and are in danger of falling into an abyss.

Freedom: Not an Indulgence

If anyone imagines that he can go over to the other side without passing through this stage [of moral perfection], he would risk making a great mistake, and of taking for perfect freedom a perfect weakness with regard to his lower nature.

It is almost impossible to pass from the mental being – even the most perfect and most remarkable – to the true spiritual life without having realised this ideal of moral perfection for a certain period of time, however brief it may be. Many people try to take a short-cut and want to assert their inner freedom before having overcome all the weaknesses of the outer nature; they are in great danger of deluding themselves. The true spiritual life, complete freedom, is something much higher than the highest moral realisations, but one must take care that this so-called freedom is not an indulgence and a contempt for all rules.

One must go higher, always higher, higher; nothing less than what the highest of humanity has achieved.

One must be capable of being spontaneously all that humanity has conceived to be the highest, the most beautiful, the most perfect, the most disinterested, the most comprehensive, the best, before opening one's spiritual wings and looking at all that from above as something which still belongs to the individual self, in order to enter into true spirituality, that which has no limits, which lives in an integral way Infinity and Eternity.

Freedom and Asceticism

To be free from all attachment does not mean running away from all occasion for attachment. All these people who assert their asceticism, not only run away but warn others not to try!

This seems so obvious to me. When you need to run away from a thing in order not to experience it, it means that you are not above it, you are still on the same level.

Anything that suppresses, diminishes or lessens cannot bring freedom. Freedom has to be experienced in the whole of life and in all sensations.

As a matter of fact I have made a whole series of studies on the subject, on the purely physical plane.... In order to be above all possible error, we tend to eliminate any occasion for error. For example, if you do not want to say any useless words, you stop speaking; people who take a vow of silence imagine that this is control of speech – it is not true! It is only eliminating the occasion for speech and therefore for saying useless things. It is the same thing with food: eating only what is necessary. . . . But the natural tendency is to fast – it is a mistake!

For fear of being mistaken in our actions, we stop doing anything at all; for fear of being mistaken in our speech, we stop speaking; for fear of eating for the pleasure of eating, we do not eat at all – this is not freedom, it is simply reducing the manifestation to a minimum; and the natural conclusion is Nirvana. But if the Lord wanted only Nirvana, nothing but Nirvana would exist! It is obvious that He conceives of the co-existence of all opposites, and that for Him this must be the beginning of a totality. So obviously, if one feels meant for that, one can choose only one of

His manifestations, that is to say, the absence of manifestation. But it is still a limitation. And this is not the only way to find Him, far from it!

It is a very common tendency which probably originates from an ancient suggestion or perhaps from some lack, some incapacity – reduce, reduce, reduce one's needs, reduce one's activities, reduce one's words, reduce one's food, reduce one's active life – and all that becomes so narrow. In one's aspiration not to make any more mistakes, one eliminates any occasion for making them. It is not a cure.

But the other way is much, much more difficult.

(Silence)

No, the solution is to act only under the divine impulsion, to speak only under the divine impulsion, to eat only under the divine impulsion. That is the difficult thing, because naturally, you immediately confuse the divine impulsion with your personal impulses.

I suppose this was the idea of all the apostles of renunciation: to eliminate everything coming from outside or from below so that if something from above should manifest one would be in a condition to receive it. But from the collective point of view, this process could take thousands of years. From the individual point of view, it is possible; but then one must keep intact the aspiration to receive the true impulsion – not the aspiration for "complete liberation", but the aspiration for *active* identification with the Supreme, that is to say, to will only what He wills, to do only what He wants: to exist by and in Him alone. So one can try the method of renunciation, but this is for one who wants to cut himself off from others. And in that case, can there be any integrality? It seems impossible to me.

To proclaim publicly what one wants to do is a considerable help. It may give rise to objections, scorn, conflict, but this is largely compensated for by public "expectation", so to say, by what other people expect from you. This was certainly the reason for those robes:[1] to let people know. Of course, that may bring you the scorn, the bad will of some people, but then there are all those who feel they must not interfere or meddle with this, that it is not their concern.

I do not know why, but it always seemed to me like showing off – it may not be and in some cases it is not, but all the same it is a way of saying to people, "Look, this is what I am." And as I say, it may help, but it has its drawbacks.

It is another childishness.

All these things are means, stages, steps, but... true freedom is to be free of everything – including means.

(*Silence*)

It is a restriction, a constriction, whereas the True Thing is an opening, a widening, an identification with the whole.

When you reduce, reduce, reduce yourself, you do not have any feeling of losing yourself, it takes away your fear of losing yourself – you become something solid and compact. But if you choose the method of widening – the greatest possible widening – you must not be afraid of losing yourself.

It is much more difficult.

Freedom and Service

Outwardly one cannot conceive how one can be at once in freedom and in servitude, but there is an attitude which reconciles the two and makes them one of the happiest states of material existence.

Freedom is a sort of instinctive need, a necessity for the integral development of the being. In its essence it is a perfect realisation of the highest consciousness, it is the expression of Unity and of union with the Divine, it is the very sense of the Origin and the

_____

1. The ochre robes of the Sannyasis.

fulfilment. But because this Unity has manifested in the many – in the multiplicity – something had to serve as a link between the Origin and the manifestation, and the most perfect link one can conceive of is love. And what is the first gesture of love? To give oneself, to serve. What is its spontaneous, immediate, inevitable movement? To serve. To serve in a joyous, complete, total self-giving.

So, in their purity, in their truth, these two things – freedom and service – far from being contradictory, are complementary. It is in perfect union with the supreme Reality that perfect freedom is found, for all ignorance, all unconsciousness is a bondage which makes you inefficient, limited, powerless. The least ignorance in oneself is a limitation, one is no longer free. As long as there is an element of unconsciousness in the being, it is a limitation, a bondage. Only in perfect union with the supreme Reality can perfect freedom exist. And how to realise this union if not through a spontaneous self-giving: the gift of love. And as I said, the first gesture, the first expression of love is service.

. . .It is indeed love which leads to Unity and it is Unity which is the true expression of freedom. And so those who in the name of their right to freedom claim independence, turn their backs completely on this true freedom, for they deny love.

Freedom and Surrender

This is what's remarkable: that when one is perfectly surrendered to the Divine one is perfectly free, and *this* is the absolute condition for freedom, to belong to the Divine alone; you are free from the whole world because you belong only to Him. And this surrender is the supreme liberation, you are also free from your little personal ego and of all things this is the most difficult – and the happiest too, the only thing that can give you a constant peace, and uninterrupted joy and the feeling of an *infinite* freedom from all that afflicts you, dwarfs, diminishes, impoverishes you, and from all that can create the least anxiety in you, the least fear. You are no longer afraid of anything, you no longer fear anything, you are the supreme master of your destiny because it is the Divine who wills in you and guides everything. But this does not happen overnight: a little time and a *great deal* of ardour in the will, not fearing to make any effort and not losing heart when one doesn't succeed, knowing that the victory is certain and that one must last out until it comes. There you are.

EFFORT, PATIENCE, PROGRESS

Go Farther

Always man takes upon his shoulders an interminable burden. He does not want to drop anything of the past and he stoops more and more under the weight of a useless accumulation.

You have a guide for a part of the way but when you have travelled this part leave the road and the guide and go farther! This is something men find difficult to do. When they get hold of something which helps them, they cling to it, they do not want to move any more. Those who have progressed with the help of Christianity do not want to give it up and they carry it on their shoulders; those who have progressed with the help of Buddhism do not want to leave it and they carry it on their shoulders, and so this hampers the advance and you are indefinitely delayed.

Once you have passed the stage, let it drop, let it go! Go farther.

Get Rid of All Ties

If your aim is to be free, in the freedom of the Spirit, you must get rid of all the ties that are not the inner truth of your being, but come from subconscious habits. If you wish to consecrate yourself entirely, absolutely and exclusively to the Divine, you must do it in all completeness; you must not leave bits of yourself tied here and there. . . .

When you come to the Yoga, you must be ready to have all your mental buildings and all your vital scaffoldings shattered to pieces. You must be prepared to be suspended in the air with nothing to support you except your faith. You will have to forget your past self and its clingings altogether, to pluck it out of your consciousness and be born anew, free from every kind of bondage. Think not of what you were, but of what you aspire to be; be altogether in what you want to realise. Turn from your dead past and look straight towards the future. Your religion, country, family lie there; it is the DIVINE.

Mental Formations and Progress

I do not believe at all in limits which cannot be crossed.

But I see very clearly people's mental formations and also a sort of laziness in face of the necessary effort. And this laziness and these limits are like diseases. But they are curable diseases.... If you are a normal person, well, provided you take the trouble and know the method, your capacity for growth is almost unlimited.

There is the idea that everyone belongs to a certain type, that, for example, the pine will never become the oak and the palm never become wheat. This is obvious. But that is something else: it means that the truth of your being is not the truth of your neighbour's. But in the truth of your being, according to your own formation, your progress is almost unlimited. It is limited only by your own conviction that it is limited and by your ignorance of the true process, otherwise...

There is nothing one cannot do, if one knows how to do it.

Preconceived Ideas

The best one can do is not to take sides, not to have preconceived ideas or principles – oh! the moral principles, the set rules of conduct, what one must do and what one must not and the preconceived ideas from the moral point of view, from the point of view of progress, and all the social and mental conventions... no worse obstacle than that. There are people, I know people who have lost decades in surmounting *one* such mental construction!... If one can be like that, open – truly open in a simplicity, well, the simplicity that knows that it is ignorant – like that (*gesture upward, of self-abandon*), ready to receive whatever comes. Then something can happen.

And naturally, the thirst for progress, the thirst for knowledge, the thirst for transformation and, above all, the thirst for Love and Truth – if one keeps that, one goes quicker. Truly a thirst, a need, a need.

All the rest has no importance; it is *that* one has need of.

The Joy of Progress

It is the will for progress and self-purification which lights the [psychic] fire. The will for progress. Those who have a strong will, when they turn it towards spiritual progress and purification, automatically light the fire within themselves.

And each defect one wants to cure or each progress one wants to make – if all that is thrown into the fire, it burns with a new intensity. And this is not an image, it is a fact in the subtle physical. One can feel the warmth of the flame, one can see in the subtle physical the light of the flame. And when there is something in the nature which prevents one from advancing and one throws it into this fire, it begins to burn and the flame becomes more intense. . . .

How can one feel sweetness and joy when one is in difficulty?

Exactly, when the difficulty is egoistic or personal, if one makes an offering of it and throws it into the fire of purification, one immediately feels the joy of progress. If one does it sincerely, at once there is a welling up of joy.

That is obviously what ought to be done instead of despairing and lamenting. If one offers it up and aspires sincerely for transformation and purification, one immediately feels joy springing up in the depths of the heart. Even when the difficulty is a great sorrow, one may do this with much success. One realises that behind the sorrow, no matter how intense it may be, there is a divine joy.

Aspire without Impatience

Aspire intensely, but without impatience.... The difference between intensity and impatience is very subtle – it is all a difference in vibration. It is subtle, but it makes all the difference.

Intensely, but without impatience. That's it. One must be in that state.

And for a very long time, a very long time, one must be satisfied with inner results, that is, results in one's personal and individual reactions, one's inner contact with the rest of the world – one must not expect or be premature in wanting things to materialise. Because our hastiness usually delays things.

If it is like that, it is like that.

We – I mean men – live harrassed lives. It is a kind of half-awareness of the shortness of their lives; they do not think of it, but they feel it half-consciously. And so they are always wanting – quick, quick, quick – to rush from one thing to another, to do one thing quickly and move on to the next one, instead of letting each thing live in its own eternity. They are always wanting: forward, forward, forward.... And the work is spoilt.

Live in Eternity

In the human consciousness everything is *very slow*. When we compare the time that is necessary to realise something with the average length of human existence, it seems interminable. But happily there comes a time when one escapes from this notion, when one begins to feel no longer according to human measures. As soon as one is truly in touch with the psychic, one loses this kind of narrowness and of agony also, this agony which is *so* bad: "I must be quick, I must be quick, there is not much time, I must hurry, there is not much time." One does things very badly or doesn't do them at all any more. But as soon as there is a contact with the psychic, then indeed this disappears; one begins to be a little more vast and calm and peaceful, and to live in eternity.

Time: a Friend or Enemy?

How is Time a friend?

It depends on how you look at it. Everything depends on the relation you have with it. If you take it as a friend, it becomes a friend. If you consider it as an enemy, it becomes your enemy.

But that's not what you are asking. What you are asking is how one feels when it is an enemy and how when it is a friend. Well, when you become impatient and tell yourself, "Oh, I must succeed in doing this and why don't I succeed in doing it?" and when you don't succeed immediately in doing it and fall into despair, then it is your enemy. But when you tell yourself, "It is all right, I didn't succeed this time, I shall succeed next time, and I am sure one day or another I shall do it", then it becomes your friend.

The Effort for Progress

Sweet Mother, when we make an effort to do better but don't see any progress, we feel discouraged. What is the best thing to do?

Not to be discouraged! Despondency leads nowhere.

To begin with, the first thing to tell yourself is that you are almost entirely incapable of knowing whether you are making progress or not, for very often what seems to us to be a state of stagnation is a long – sometimes long, but in any case not endless – preparation for a leap forward. We sometimes seem to be marking time for weeks or months, and then suddenly something that was being prepared makes its appearance, and we see that there is quite a considerable change and *on several points* at a time.

As with everything in yoga, the effort for progress must be made for the love of the effort for progress. The joy of effort, the aspiration for progress must be enough in themselves, quite independent of the result. Everything one does in yoga must be done for the joy of doing it, and not in view of the result one wants to obtain.... Indeed, in life, always, in all things, the result does not belong to us. And if we want to keep the right attitude, we must act, feel, think, strive spontaneously, for *that* is what we must do, and not in view of the result to be obtained.

As soon as we think of the result we begin to bargain and that takes away all sincerity from the effort. You make an effort to progress because you feel within you the need, the *imperative* need to make an effort and progress; and this effort is the gift you offer to the Divine Consciousness in you, the Divine Consciousness in the Universe, it is your way of expressing your gratitude, offering your self; and whether this results in progress or not is of no importance. You will progress when it is decided that the time has come to progress and not because you desire it.

Horizontal and Vertical Progress

There is a horizontal advance between abrupt ascents. It is the moment of the abrupt ascent which gives you an impression of something like a revelation, a great inner joy. But once you have climbed the step, if you want to climb it once more you would have to go down again. You must go on preparing yourself at this level in order to climb another higher step. These things which suddenly give you a great joy are always ascents. But these ascents are prepared by a slow work of horizontal progress, that is, one must become more and more conscious, establish more and more perfectly what one is, draw from it all the inner, psychological consequences, and in action also. It is a long utilisation of an abrupt leap and, as I say, there are two kinds of progress. But the horizontal progress is indispensable.

You must not stop, you must not cling in this way to your vertical progress and not want to move because it has brought you a revelation. You must know how to leave it in order to prepare for another.

True Progress

We are upon earth; the period one passes on earth is that in which one can make progress. One does not progress outside terrestrial life. The earthly, material existence is essentially the life of progress, it is here that one makes progress. Outside the earthly life one takes rest or is unconscious or one may have periods of assimilation, periods of rest, periods of unconsciousness. But as for the periods of progress, they are on earth and in the body. So, when you take a body it is to make progress, and when you leave it the period of progress is over.

And true progress is sadhana; that is, it is the most conscious and swiftest progress. Otherwise one makes progress with the rhythm of Nature, which means that it can take centuries and centuries and centuries and millenniums to make the slightest bit of progress. But true progress is that made by sadhana. In yoga one can do in a very short time what takes otherwise an interminable time. But it is always in the body and always upon earth that it is done, not elsewhere. That is why when one is in a body one must take advantage of it and not waste one's time, not say, "A little later, a little later." It is much better to do it immediately. All the years you pass without making any progress are wasted years which you are sure to regret afterwards.

You Must Choose

You must choose; there is no "force like that" which chooses for you, or chance or luck or fate – this is not true. Your will is free, it is deliberately left free and you have to choose. It is you who decide whether to seek the Light or not, whether to be the servitor of the Truth or not – it is you. Or whether to have an aspiration or not, it is you who choose. And even when you are told, "Make your surrender total and the work will be done for you", it is quite all right, but to make your surrender total, every day and at every moment you must choose to make your surrender total, otherwise you will not do it, it will not get done by itself. It is you who must want to do it. When it is done, all goes well, when you have the Knowledge also, all goes well, and when you are identified with the Divine, all goes even better, but till then you must will, choose and decide. Don't go to sleep lazily, saying, "Oh! the work will be done for me, I have nothing to do but let myself glide along with the stream." Besides, it is not true, the work is not done by itself, because if the least little thing thwarts your little will, it says, "No, not that!..." Then?

Nothing Is Done Until Everything Is Done

In the old Chaldean tradition, very often the young novices were given an image when they were invested with the white robe; they were told: "Do not try to remove the stains one by one, the whole robe must be purified." Do not try to correct your faults one by one, to overcome your weaknesses one by one, it does not take you very far. The entire consciousness must be changed, a reversal of consciousness must be achieved, a springing up out of the state in which one is towards a higher state from which one dominates all the weaknesses one wants to heal, and from which one has a full vision of the work to be accomplished.

I believe Sri Aurobindo has said this: things are such that it may be said that nothing is done until everything is done. One step ahead is not enough, a total conversion is necessary.

How many times have I heard people who were making an effort say, "I try, but what's the use of my trying? Every time I think I have gained something, I find that I must begin all over again." This happens because they are trying to go forward while standing still, they are trying to progress without changing their consciousness. It is the entire point of view which must be shifted, the whole consciousness must get out of the rut in which it lies so as to rise up and see things from above. It is only thus that victories will not be changed into defeats.

"Others Are Not Doing It"

What prevents me from opening myself to the [Divine's] influence is the suggestion, "Why hurry, why so soon, since the others are not doing it?"

This is a frightful platitude!

But even if you must be the one and only being in the whole creation who gives himself integrally in all purity to the Divine, and being the only one, being naturally absolutely misunderstood by everybody, scoffed at, ridiculed, hated, even if you were that, there is no reason for not doing it. One must be either a tinsel actor or else a fool. Because others don't do it? But what does it matter whether they do it or not? "Why, the whole world may go the wrong way, it does not concern me. There is only one thing with which I am concerned, to go straight. What others do, how is it my concern? It is their business, not mine."

This is the worst of all slaveries!

Your Best Friend

Your friend is not one who encourages you to come down to your lowest level, encourages you to do foolish things along with him or fall into bad ways with him or one who commends you for all the nasty things you do, that's quite clear. . . .

We don't like the company of someone who has a contagious disease, and avoid him carefully; generally he is segregated so that it does not spread. But the contagion of vice and bad behaviour, the contagion of depravity, falsehood and what is base, is infinitely more dangerous than the contagion of any disease, and this is what must be very carefully avoided. You must consider as your best friend the one who tells you that he does not wish to participate in any bad or ugly act, the one who gives you courage to resist low temptations; he is a friend. He is the one you must associate with and not someone with whom you have fun and who strengthens your evil propensities. That's all.

Now, we won't labour the point and I hope that those I have in mind will understand what I have said.

Indeed, you should choose as friends only those who are wiser than yourself, those whose company ennobles you and helps you to master yourself, to progress, to act in a better way and see more clearly. And finally, the best friend one can have – isn't he the Divine, to whom one can say everything, reveal everything? For there indeed is the source of all compassion, of all power to efface every error when it is not repeated, to open the road to true realisation; it is he who can understand all, heal all, and always help on the path, help you not to fail, not to falter, not to fall, but to walk straight to the goal. He is the true friend, the friend of good and bad days, the one who can understand, can heal, and who is always there when you need him. When you call him sincerely, he is always there to guide and uphold you – and to love you in the true way.

THE DIVINE, THE WORLD AND MAN

Rely on the Divine Alone

There is one thing you must learn, never to rely on anyone or anything whatever except the Divine. For if you lean upon anyone for support, that support will break, you may be sure of that. From the minute you start doing yoga (I always speak of those who do yoga, I do not speak about ordinary life), for those who do yoga, to depend upon someone else is like wanting to transform that person into a representative of the Divine Force; now you may be sure there is not one in a hundred million who can carry the weight: he will break immediately. So never take the attitude of hoping for support, help, comfort from anyone except the Divine. That is absolute; I have never, not once, met anyone who tried to cling to something to find a support there (someone doing yoga or who has been put into touch with yoga) and who was not deceived – it breaks, it stops, one loses one's support. Then one says, "Life is difficult" – it is not difficult but one must know what one is doing. Never seek a support elsewhere than in the Divine. Never seek satisfaction elsewhere than in the Divine. Never seek the satisfaction of your needs in anyone else except the Divine – never, for anything at all. All your needs can be satisfied only by the Divine. All your weaknesses can be borne and healed only by the Divine. He alone is capable of giving you what you need in everything, always, and if you try to find any satisfaction or support or help or joy or... Heaven knows what, in anyone else, you will always fall on your nose one day, and that always hurts, sometimes even hurts very much.

Ask the Divine

If, for example, one wants to know something or one needs guidance, or something else, how can one have it from the Divine, according to one's need?

By asking the Divine for it. If you do not ask Him, how can you have it?

If you turn to the Divine and have full trust and ask Him, you will get what you need – not necessarily what you imagine you need; but the true thing you need, you will get. But you must ask Him for it.

You must make the experiment sincerely; you must not endeavour to get it by all sorts of external means and then expect the Divine to give it to you, without even having asked Him. Indeed, when you want somebody to give you something, you ask him for it, don't you? And why do you expect the Divine to give it to you without your having asked Him for it?

Finding the Divine

Sweet Mother, how can we find the Divine who is hidden in us?

This we have explained many, many times. But the first thing is to want it, and know precisely that this comes first, before all other things, that this is the important thing. That is the first condition; all the rest may come later, this is the *essential* condition. You see, if once in a while, from time to time, when you have nothing to do and all goes well and you are unoccupied, suddenly you tell yourself, "Ah, I would like so much to find the Divine!" – well, this – it may take a hundred thousand years, in this way.

But if it is the important thing, the only thing that matters, and if everything else comes afterwards, and you want nothing *but this*, then – this is the first condition. You must first establish this, later we may speak of what follows. First this, that all the rest does not count, that only *this* counts, that one is ready to give up everything to have this, that it is the only thing of importance in life. Then one puts oneself in the condition of being able to take a step forward.

Knowing the Divine

Do you understand, the only way of knowing the Divine is by identifying oneself with Him. There is no other, there is only one, one single way. Hence, once you are master of this method of identification, you can identify yourself. So you choose your object for identification, you want to identify yourself with the Divine. But so long as you do not know how to identify yourself, a hundred and one things will always come across your path, pulling you here, pulling you there, scattering you, and you will not be able to identify yourself with Him. But if you have learnt how to identify yourself, then you have only to orient the identification, place it where you want it, and then hold on there until you get a result. It will come very fast if you are master of your power of identification. Yes, it will come very quickly. Ramakrishna used to say that the time could vary between three days, three hours and three minutes. Three days for very slow people, three hours for those who were a little swifter, three minutes for those who are used to it.

God Has a Sense of Humour

Someone has asked me, "How is it possible for God to reveal Himself to an unbeliever?" That's very funny; because if it pleases God to reveal Himself to an unbeliever, I don't see what would prevent Him from doing so!

On the contrary, He has a sense of humour – Sri Aurobindo has told us many times already that the Supreme has a sense of humour, that *we* are the ones who want to make Him into a grave and invariably serious character – and He may find it very amusing to come and embrace an unbeliever. Someone who has only the day before declared, "God does not exist. I do not believe in Him. All that is folly and ignorance....", He gathers him into His arms, He presses him to His heart – and He laughs in his face.

Everything is possible, even things which to our small and limited intelligence seem absurd.

The Atheist and the Believer

"The Atheist is God playing at hide and seek with Himself; but is the Theist any other? Well, perhaps; for he has seen the shadow of God and clutched at it."
             Sri Aurobindo, Thoughts and Aphorisms

What does "God playing at hide and seek with Himself" mean?

In the game of hide and seek, one person hides and the other seeks. So God hides from the atheist who says, "God? I do not see him, I do not know where he is; therefore he does not exist." But the atheist does not know that God is also in him; and therefore it is God who is denying his own existence. Isn't that a game? And yet a day will come when he will be brought face to face with himself and will be obliged to recognise that he exists.

The believer thinks himself very superior to the atheist, but all that he has been able to seize of God is His shadow and he clings to this shadow imagining that it is God himself. For if he truly knew God, he would know that God is all things and in everything; then he would cease to think himself superior to anybody.

The Material World

Is not this material world of ours very low down in the scale in the system of worlds that form the creation?

Ours is the most material world, but it is not necessarily "low down", at least, not for that reason; if it is low down, it is because it is obscure and ignorant, not because it is material. It is a mistake to make "matter" a synonym for obscurity and ignorance. And the material world too is not the only world in which we live: it is rather one of many in which we exist simultaneously, and in one way the most important of them all. For this world of matter is the point of concentration of all the worlds; it is the field of concretisa-

tion of all the worlds; it is the place where all the worlds will have
to manifest. At present it is disharmonious and obscure; but that is
only an accident, a false start. One day it will become beautiful,
rhythmic, full of light; for that is the consummation for which it
was made.

The Divine Is Not a Stranger

*But why does the Divine want to manifest Himself on earth in this
chaos?*

Because this is why He has created the earth, not for any other
motive; the earth is He Himself in a deformation and He wants to
establish it back again in its truth. Earth is not something
separated from Him and alien to Him. It is a deformation of
Himself which must once again become what it was in its essence,
that is, the Divine.

Then why is He a stranger to us?

But He is not a stranger, my child. You fancy that He is a stranger,
but He is not, not in the least. He is the essence of your being – not
at all alien. You may not know Him, but He is not a stranger; He is
the very essence of your being. Without the Divine you would not
exist. Without the Divine you could not exist even for the
millionth part of a second.

God and His Creation

People are so deeply imbued with the Christian idea of "God the
Creator" – the creation on one side and God on the other. When
you think about it you reject it, but it has penetrated into the
sensations and feelings; so, spontaneously, instinctively, almost
subconsciously, you attribute to God everything you consider to

be best and most beautiful and, above all, everything you want to attain, to realise. Naturally, each one changes the content of his God according to his own consciousness, but it is always what he considers to be best. And that is also why instinctively and spontaneously, subconsciously, you are shocked by the idea that God can be things that you do not like, that you do not approve of or do not think best.

I put that rather childishly, on purpose, so that you can understand it properly. But it is like that – I am sure, because I observed it in myself for a very long time, because of the subconscious formation of childhood, environment, education, etc. You must be able to press into this body the consciousness of Oneness, the absolute exclusive Oneness of the Divine – exclusive in the sense that nothing exists except in this Oneness, even the things we find most repulsive. . . .

But it is Him. There is nothing but Him. This is what we should repeat to ourselves from morning to evening and from evening to morning, because we forget it at each moment.

There is only Him. There is nothing but Him – He alone exists, there is no existence without Him, there is only Him!

God and the Universe

There is only one single solution to the problem – not to make any distinction between God and the universe at the origin. The universe *is* the Divine projected in space, and God *is* the universe at its origin. It is the same thing under one aspect or another. And you cannot divide them. It is the opposite conception to that of the "creator" and his "work". Only, it is very convenient to speak of the creator and his work, it makes explanations very easy and the teaching quite elementary. But it is not the truth. And then you say: "How is it that God who is all-powerful has allowed the world to be like this?" But it is your own conception! It is because you yourself happen to be in the midst of a set of circumstances that seems to you unpleasant, so you project that upon the Divine and you tell him: "Why have you made such a world?" – "I did not make it. It is you yourself. And if you become Myself once again, you will no longer feel as you do. What makes you feel as you do is that you are no longer Myself." This is what He could tell you in answer. And the fact is that when you succeed in uniting your consciousness with the divine consciousness, there is no problem left. Everything appears quite natural and simple and all right and exactly what it had to be.

The Lord Is Staging a Play

If one looks attentively, one has to think that the Lord is staging a fantastic play for Himself! That the Manifestation is a play which He is acting for Himself and with Himself.

He has taken the stand of the spectator and He looks at Himself. And so in order to look at Himself, He must accept the concept of time and space, otherwise He cannot! And immediately the whole comedy begins. But it is a comedy, nothing more.

But we take it seriously, because we are puppets! But as soon as we stop being puppets, we can see quite clearly that it is a comedy.

For some people it is also a real tragedy.

Yes, we are the ones who make it tragic. *We are the ones* who make it tragic. . . .

You see, only the one who is watching the play is not worried, because he knows everything that is going to happen and he has an absolute knowledge of everything – everything that happens, everything that has happened and everything that is going to happen – and it is all there, as *one* presence for him. And so it is the others, the poor actors who do not even know, they do not even know their parts! And they worry a great deal, because they are being made to act something and they do not know what it is. This is something I have just been feeling very strongly: we are all acting a play, but we do not know what the play is, nor where it is going, nor where it comes from, nor what it is as a whole; we barely know – imperfectly – what we are supposed to do from moment to moment. Our knowledge is imperfect. And so we worry! But when one knows everything, one can no longer worry, one smiles – He must be having great fun, but we... And yet we are given the *full power* to amuse ourselves like Him.

We simply do not take the trouble.

The Lord Plays with All This

When one has the positive experience of the one and only existence of the Supreme and that all is only the Supreme playing to Himself, instead of being something disquieting or unpleasant or troubling, it is on the contrary a sort of total security.

The one reality is the Supreme. And all this is a game He plays to Himself. I find this much more comforting than the opposite view.

And after all, this is the only certitude that all this may become something marvellous. . . .

You will see, there is a moment when one cannot bear oneself or life unless one takes the attitude that it is the Lord who is everything. You see, this Lord, how many things He possesses, He plays with all this – He plays, He plays at changing the positions. And so, when one sees this, this whole, one feels the illimitable marvel, and that all our most wonderful aspirations, all these are quite possible and will even be surpassed. Then one is comforted. Otherwise, existence... it is inconsolable. . . .

The present way of being is a past which truly should no longer be there. While the other: "Ah! at last! at last! it is for this that there is a world."

And everything else remains quite as concrete and real – it does not become hazy! It is just as concrete, just as real, but... but it becomes divine, because... because it *is* the Divine. It is the Divine who plays.

Allow the Lord to Do Everything

Now, when I start looking like this (*Mother closes her eyes*), two
things are there at the same time: this smile, this joy, this laughter
are there, and such peace! Such *full*, luminous, total peace, in
which there are no more conflicts, no more contradictions. There
are no more conflicts. It is *one single* luminous harmony – and yet
everything we call error, suffering, misery, everything is there. *It
eliminates nothing*. It is another way of seeing.

(*Long silence*)

There can be no doubt that if you sincerely want to get out of it,
it is not so difficult after all: you have nothing to do, you only have
to allow the Lord to do everything. And He does everything. He
does everything. It is so wonderful, so wonderful!

He takes anything, even what we call a very ordinary intelligence and he simply teaches you to put this intelligence aside, to
rest: "There, be quiet, don't stir, don't bother me, I don't need
you." Then a door opens – you don't even feel that you have to
open it; it is wide open, you are taken over to the other side. All
that is done by Someone else, not you. And then the other way
becomes impossible.

All this... oh, this tremendous labour of the mind striving to
understand, toiling and giving itself headaches!... It is absolutely
useless, absolutely useless, no use at all, it merely increases the
confusion.

You are faced with a so-called problem: what should you say,
what should you do, how should you act? There is nothing to do,
nothing, you only have to say to the Lord, "There, You see, it is
like that" – that's all. And then you stay very quiet. And then quite
spontaneously, without thinking about it, without reflection,
without calculation, nothing, nothing, without the slightest effort
– you do what has to be done. That is to say, the Lord does it, it is
no longer you. He does it, He arranges the cirmumstances, He
arranges the people, He puts the words into your mouth or your

pen – He does everything, everything, everything, everything; you have nothing more to do but to allow yourself to live blissfully.

I am more and more convinced that people do not really want it.

But clearing the ground is difficult, the work of clearing the ground beforehand.

But you don't even need to do it! He does it for you.

But they are constantly breaking in: the old consciousness, the old thoughts....

Yes, they try to come in again, by habit. You only have to say, "Lord, You see, You see, You see, it is like that" – that's all. "Lord, You see, You see this, You see that, You see this fool" – and it is all over immediately. And it changes automatically, my child, without the slightest effort. Simply to be sincere, that is to say, to *truly* want everything to be right. You are perfectly conscious that you can do nothing about it, that you have no capacity. . . . But there is always something that wants to do it by itself; that's the trouble, otherwise...

No, you may be full of an excellent goodwill and then *you want* to do it. That's what complicates everything. Or else you don't have faith, you believe that the Lord will not be able to do it and that you must do it yourself, because He does not know! (*Mother laughs.*) This, this kind of stupidity is very common. "How can He see things? We live in a world of Falsehood, how can He see Falsehood and see..." But He sees the thing as it is! Exactly!

I am not speaking of people of no intelligence, I am speaking of people who are intelligent and who try – there is a kind of conviction, like that, somewhere, even in people who know that we live in a world of Ignorance and Falsehood and that there is a Lord who is All-Truth. They say, "Precisely because He is All-Truth, He does not understand. (*Mother laughs.*) He does not understand our falsehood, I must deal with it myself." That is very strong, very common.

Ah! we make complications for nothing.

Let the All-Consciousness Decide

I am fully convinced that the confusion [in the world] is there to
teach us how to live from day to day, that is to say, not to be
preoccupied with what may happen, what will happen, just to
occupy oneself day by day with doing what one has to do. All
thinkings, pre-plannings, arrangements and all that, are very
favourable to much disorder.

To live almost minute by minute, to be like that (*gesture
upward*), attentive only to the thing that is to be done at the
moment, and then to let the All-Consciousness decide.... We can
never know things even with the widest vision: we can know things
only *very* partially – very partially. So our attention is drawn this
way and that, and still other things are there. By giving great
importance to things dangerous and harmful, you only add
strength to them.

(*Mother goes into contemplation.*)

When you are assailed by the vision of such disorder and
confusion, you have to do only one thing, to enter into the
consciousness where you see only *one* Being, *one* Consciousness,
one Power – there is only a single Unity – and all this is taking place
within this Unity. And all our insignificant visions and knowings
and judgments and... all that is mere nothing, it is microscopic in
comparison with the Consciousness presiding over All. Therefore,
if one had the least sense of the reason why separate individualities
existed, one would see that it was only for allowing aspiration, the
existence of aspiration, of this movement of self-giving and
surrender, trust and *faith*. And it is this that is the very reason why
individuals were built up; and then, for you to become that in all
sincerity and intensity... it is all that is needed.

It is all that is needed, it is the *only* thing, the only thing that
stays; all the rest... phantasmagoria.

And it is the only thing valid in every case: when you want to do
a thing, when you cannot do a thing, when you move, when the

body is no more able to move... in *every*, every case, that only, only that: to come in conscious contact with the Supreme Consciousness, to be united with it; and... to wait. There!

It is then that you receive the exact indication of what you ought to do at each minute – to do or not to do, to act or to be stone still. That is all. And even to be or not to be. That is the only solution. More and more, more and more, the certitude is there: this is the *only* solution. All the rest is mere childishness.

"What Thou Willest"

Is it enough to let oneself be filled with That, is there nothing else to do?

I think, I think that it is the only thing. I am repeating always: "What Thou willest, what Thou willest, what Thou willest... let it be what Thou willest, may I do what Thou willest, may I be conscious of what Thou willest."

And also: "Without Thee it is death; with Thee it is life." By "death" I do not mean physical death – it may be so; it may be that now if I lost the contact, that would be the end, but it is impossible! I have the feeling that it is... that I *am That* – with all the obstructions that the present consciousness may still have, that's all. And then, when I see someone (*Mother opens her hands as though to offer the person to the Light*), whoever he may be: like that (*same gesture*).

(Silence)

All the while (it is amusing), all the while I have the feeling that I am a little baby who nestles – nestles within... (what to call it?) a Divine Consciousness... *all-embracing*.

The Pressure of the Consciousness

You know, I do not believe in external decisions. I simply believe
in one thing only: the force of the Consciousness which is making a
pressure like that (*crushing gesture*). And the pressure goes on
increasing... which means that it will sift out the people. I believe
only in that – the pressure of the Consciousness. All the rest are
things that men do. They do them more or less well, and then it
lives, and then it dies, and then it changes, and then it gets
distorted, and then... everything they have done. It is not worth
the trouble. The power of execution must come from above, like
that, imperative (*gesture of descent*)! And for that, this (*Mother
points to her forehead*), this must keep quiet. Not to say, "Oh, that
must not be, oh! this must be, oh! we ought to do..." Peace, peace,
peace. He knows better than you what is needed.

A SKETCH OF THE MOTHER'S LIFE

The Mother was born in Paris on 21 February 1878. Mirra, as the child was named, was the daughter of Maurice Alfassa, a banker born in Adrianople, Turkey, in 1843, and Mathilde Ismaloun, born in Alexandria, Egypt, in 1857. Maurice, his wife and their son, Mattéo, born in Alexandria in 1876, emigrated from Egypt to France in 1877, one year before Mirra's birth. Her early education was given at home. About the age of fourteen she attended a studio to learn drawing and painting, and later studied at the famous École de Beaux Arts. Besides being an accomplished painter (some of her works were exhibited at the Paris Salon), the Mother was a talented musican and writer.

Concerning her early spiritual life, the Mother has written: "Between eleven and thirteen a series of psychic and spiritual experiences revealed to me not only the existence of God but man's possibility of uniting with Him, of realising Him integrally in a life divine." Around 1905, while in her mid-twenties, the Mother voyaged to Tlemcen, Algeria, where she studied occultism for two years with a Polish or Russian adept, Max Théon, and his wife. Returning to Paris in 1906, she founded her first group of spiritual seekers. Between 1911 and 1913 she gave many talks to various groups in Paris.

At the age of thirty-six the Mother sailed to Pondicherry, India, to meet Sri Aurobindo. She saw him on 29 March 1914 and at once recognised him as the one who for many years had inwardly guided her spiritual development. She remained in Pondicherry for eleven months, but was then obliged to return to France due to the outbreak of the First World War. After a year in France, she went to Japan and stayed for a period of nearly four years.

On 24 April 1920 the Mother returned to Pondicherry and resumed her collaboration with Sri Aurobindo. With her coming, the number of disciples around Sri Aurobindo gradually increased. This informal grouping eventually took shape as the Sri Aurobindo Ashram. From its inception in November 1926, Sri Aurobindo entrusted the full material and spiritual charge of the

Ashram to the Mother. Under her guidance, which covered a span of nearly fifty years, the Ashram grew into a large, many-facetted community which today numbers about 1200 persons; there are, in addition, several hundred others who live in the same area (the "French section" of Pondicherry). In 1943 the Mother started a small school which gradually expanded to become the Sri Aurobindo International Centre of Education; inaugurated on 6 January 1952, the Centre presently has around 450 students. The Mother also initiated an international township, Auroville, the "City of Dawn", which is located eight kilometres from Pondicherry. It was founded on 28 February 1968. About 500 persons from India and abroad currently live in Auroville.

The Mother participated in the daily activities of the Ashram until the age of eighty-four. In March 1962 she retired to her rooms, but from there continued, during the next decade, to guide the Ashram and to receive people regularly. On 17 November 1973, at the age of ninety-five, the Mother left her body.

About the relationship between the Mother and himself, Sri Aurobindo has written: "The Mother's consciousness and mine are the same", and again: "There is no difference between the Mother's path and mine; we have and have always had the same path, the path that leads to the supramental change and the divine realisation. . . ."

The Mother, on her ninetieth birthday, summarised her life and work in this way: "The reminiscences will be short.

"I came to India to meet Sri Aurobindo, I remained in India to live with Sri Aurobindo. When he left his body, I continued to live here in order to do his work which is, by serving the Truth and enlightening mankind, to hasten the rule of the Divine's Love upon earth."

REFERENCES TO THE TEXTS

The passages for this book have been selected from the following volumes of the Mother's Collected Works, published by the Sri Aurobindo Ashram, Pondicherry.

Volume	Title	Publication Date
3	*Questions and Answers*	1977
4	*Questions and Answers 1950-51*	1972
5	*Questions and Answers 1953*	1976
6	*Questions and Answers 1954*	1979
7	*Questions and Answers 1955*	1979
8	*Questions and Answers 1956*	1979
9	*Questions and Answers 1957-58*	1977
10	*On Thoughts and Aphorisms*	1977
11	*Notes on the Way*	1980
12	*On Education*	1978
13	*Words of the Mother [1]*	1980
15	*Words of the Mother [3]*	1980

All but five passages are extracts from conversations. The five, which are written statements, are published in Volume 10 on pages 55-56, 57, 57-58, 58-59 and 96-97.

Ninety percent of the material was originally spoken (in five cases, written) in French. The ten percent spoken in English is published in Volume 3 between pages 1-180 and in Volume 15 on pages 419-23.

The references begin on the next page.

The references below are given in an abbreviated form. A number set in **bold face type** indicates the **page number of this book** on which a given passage begins. The subsequent numbers, which are in roman type face, indicate the source from which the passage was taken: that is, the Centenary Volume and page number(s). Thus, for example, in the first reference below, the abbreviation "**1**: 9:150-51, 7:327" means that on page 1 of this book, the first passage is taken from Collected Works Volume 9, pages 150-51, the second from Volume 7, page 327.

The references follow:

1: 9:150-51, 7:327. **2**: 9:74. **3**: 9:161-62. **4**: 6:151-52. **5**: 6:261, 6:317-18. **6**: 9:100-02, 7:173-74. **7**: 7:58-59. **8**: 6:412-13. **9**: 4:49-50. **10**: 7:38-40, 5:19-20. **11**: 5:303-04. **12**: 3:118-19. **13**: 8:143. **14**: 5:12-15. **16**: 3:76-78. **17**: 8:147. **18**: 10:96-97. **19**: 200-03. **20**: 3:1. **21**: 3:4-5, 3:126. **22**: 3:114-15. **23**: 4:373. **24**: 3:23-24. **25**: 5:44-45. **26**: 6:428-29. **27**: 6:301-02, 5:46. **28**: 5:285-86, 3:133. **30**: 8:248-49, 6:132-33. **31**: 6:215-16. **32**: 5:10, 8:308-09. **33**: 11:211-12. **34**: 8:22. **35**: 3:202, 6:329-30. **36**: 5:214-15. **37**: 4:359-60. **38**: 6:350, 10:55-56. **39**: 6:343-44, 8:294. **40**: 6:391. **41**: 6:348. **42**: 10:21-23. **43**: 4:368-69. **44**: 3:264-65, 15:419-21. **46**: 7:245. **47**: 6:213, 3:160. **48**: 3:34-35. **49**: 5:95-96, 7:18. **51**: 8:261-62, 4:211-12. **52**: 6:50, 7:31. **53**: 9:40-41, 10:57-58. **54**: 6:323-24, 4:181. **55**: 8:42. **56**: 9:70-71, 4:31-32. **58**: 7:137-38. **59**: 7:140, 142. **60**: 6:82. **61**: 6:112. **62**: 6:113, 6:115-16. **63**: 9:374-75. **64**: 7:239. **65**: 9:360-61. **66**: 4:5, 9:114-15. **67**: 8:89, 3:20-21. **68**: 4:121-22. **69**: 9:81-82. **70**: 13:319-20, 3:25-26. **71**: 7:407-08, 7:415-16. **72**: 7:191-92. **73**: 6:155-56. **74**: 6:269. **75**: 3:66-67, 9:423-24. **76**: 6:313-14. **77**: 3:250-51. **78**: 6:344-345. **79**: 6:328-29. **81**: 6:432. **82**: 4:64, 6:25-27. **84**: 9:431, 7:195:96. **86**: 7:273, 3:62-63. **87**: 3:7. **88**: 8:176, 6:160. **89**: 7:21. **90**: 15:326, 3:152. **91**: 6:138-39. **92**: 7:399-401. **93**: 6:136-37, 6:332-33. **94**: 6:390-91. **95**: 6:137-38. **96**: 9:241-42, 5:233-34. **97**: 7:247. **98**: 4:117, 3:19. **99**: 3:8-9. **100**: 4:208, 9:30. **102**: 6:349, 6:394-95. **103**: 6:403-04. **104**: 9:351-52. **105**: 8:251, 6:322-23. **106**: 6:217. **107**: 8:84-85. **108**: 8:396-97. **109**: 6:22-23. **110**: 3:215, 3:156-57. **111**: 7:233, 3:198, 200. **112**: 6:356-57. **114**: 6:18-19. **115**: 6:430-32. **116**:

GLOSSARY OF SANSKRIT AND OTHER TERMS

The following definitions are based upon the writings of Sri Aurobindo.

Adverse (hostile) forces — not merely undivine but anti-divine forces.

Mantra — sacred syllable, name or mystic formula; set words or sounds having a spiritual significance and power.

Mind (the mental) — the part of the nature which has to do with cognition and intelligence, with ideas, with mental or thought perceptions, the reactions of thought to things, with the truly mental movements and formations, mental vision and will, etc. that are part of man's intelligence.

Psychic being — the evolving soul; the soul of the individual evolving in the manifestation; the soul-individuality. The term "soul" is sometimes used as a synonym for "psychic being", but, strictly regarded, there is a distinction. The soul is the divine essence in the individual, the psychic being is the developing soul-personality put forth by the soul as its representative in the evolution. This psychic being evolves and grows by its experiences in the manifestation; as it develops, it increasingly aids the evolution and growth of the mental, vital and physical parts of the being.

Puja — worship.

Rajasic — of the nature of Rajas, one of the three qualities or modes of Nature. Rajas is the force of kinesis and translates in quality as struggle and effort, passion and action.

Sadhak — one who practises a spiritual discipline; one who is getting or trying to get spiritual realisation.

Sadhana — spiritual practice or discipline; the practice of yoga.

Sannyasin — one who has renounced the world and action; an ascetic.

Sattwic — of the nature of Sattwa, one of the three qualities or modes of Nature. Sattwa is the force of equilibrium and translates in quality as good and harmony and happiness and light.

Soul — the divine essence in the individual; the essential psychic existence; the divine spark which supports from its place behind the heart-centre the mental, vital, physical, psychic evolution of the being in Nature. The soul is a portion of the Divine descended into the evolution as a divine Principle within it to support the evolution of the individual. The term "soul" is sometimes used as a synonym for "psychic being".

Spirit — the Consciousness above mind, the Self which is always in oneness with the Divine; self-existent being with an infinite power of consciousness and unconditioned delight in its being.

Supermind (the Supramental) — the Truth-Consciousness, a principle of active Will and Knowledge superior to Mind; it exists, acts and proceeds in the fundamental truth and unity of things.

Tamas — one of the three qualities or modes of Nature. Tamas is the force of inconscience and inertia and translates in quality as incapacity and inaction.

Tapasya — energism, austerity of personal will; concentration of the will and energy to control the mind, vital and physical and change them or bring down the higher consciousness or for any yogic or higher purpose.

Transformation — means that the higher consciousness or nature is brought down into the mind, vital and body and takes the place of the lower.

Vital — the Life-nature made up of desires, sensations, feelings, passions, energies of action, will of desire, reactions of the desire-soul of man and of all that play of possessive and other related instincts, anger, greed, lust, etc., that belong to this field of the nature.

Yoga — union with the Self, the Spirit or the Divine; the discipline by which one seeks deliberately and consciously to attain that union or, more generally, to attain a higher consciousness. Yoga is a generic name for the processes and the result of processes by which one transcends one's present modes of being and rises to a new, a higher, a wider mode of consciousness.

Yogi — one who practices yoga; but especially, one who is already
established in spiritual realisation, one who has attained the
goal of yoga.